La Paracléte:

The Story of Abelard and Héloïse

by

Rod Randall

Edited by Roxane Christ

authorHOUSE™

1663 LIBERTY DRIVE, SUITE 200
BLOOMINGTON, INDIANA 47403
(800) 839-8640
WWW.AUTHORHOUSE.COM

First published by AuthorHouse 03/25/05

ISBN: 1-4208-1080-4 (sc)
ISBN: 1-4208-1081-2 (dj)

Library of Congress Control Number: 2004098894

Printed in the United States of America
Bloomington, Indiana

This book is printed on acid-free paper.

*To those whose spirits have
intertwined with mine*

Prologue

Exhumation ad initium

*D*eath cannot conquer love.
The grave cannot contain it.

"It has been over twenty years since last I stepped foot on this soil. Without tears I had watched the ground open up and swallow him. Pierre Abelard had been my friend, and, although this friendship was turbulent, it enriched me."

The old man speaking, whom I knew so well, was just one shadowy figure among several haunting silhouettes cast against the gloom of this night. Some of these outlines were caused by members of this world while others, I imagined, defined incorporeal personages assembled to witness this ultimate event.

"But as his corpse disappeared beneath the dark, damp dirt, so, too, disappeared further thought of him," stated the old man as he continued his dissertation. "Bernard was right. Abelard was a mediocre scholar. Without his own charismatic and imposing presence, his theological views could neither withstand the scrutiny of his peers nor the judgment of posterity. How often it is an individual who brings superficial

1

validity to his ideas through charm, enthusiasm, or physical appeal. Yet, those ideas can be critically shredded when considered without prejudice. I am sorry to say I feel this was the case with Abelard."

Due to the improper nature of this interment it was being executed under the cover of night and without ceremony. The silent facades of the few tombstones, which were being strangled by an overgrowth of vines that appeared to be squeezing the very life out of the rock, seemed appropriate by their cold, pale, and bloodless indifference to this dark episode.

I had arrived late, toward the end of the task. My approach to this cemetery plot from the other side of the impoverished convent of La Paracléte seemed to arouse unnatural nervousness among the small band that had gathered to participate in this staid occasion. One of the labourers stopped his illicit work and left the scene out of worry that I might be some worldly, or unworldly, authority coming to exact due punishment on him for such a vain desecration.

At my imminent arrival the old man had remained the most composed of the group. With difficulty, he had risen erect from a kneeling position at the graveside to meet the intruder. With a strong shudder, he seemed to shrug off the pervasive moodiness of the moment to take a firm stance in my direction. He peered intently into the darkness although I was nearly in reach and only a few feet away. I sensed in him that four score of years had weakened the body, but they had not weakened the will.

Finally, he identified the interloper. "You are tardy as always," he said in a familiar, yet gentle, reprimand. "You are a man of forty years yet still have little regard for the precept of punctuality." The old man put a trembling hand upon the side of my face and noted, "Ah, the blush of youth still lingers on your cheek. Your eyes glisten in evidence of the brightness inside you. From whence are you so sustained? I greet you with joy even at this sombre time."

He moved a short distance to a gravestone that was being lit by a focused beam of starlight to begin his account. As he rested heavily against the solid monument, that solitary stream of silver light, which had somehow managed to pierce the smothering cloud cover, landed upon his face. For an instant, it caused a sparkle in the eye of this life-weary sojourner, but reflexively averting himself from its brilliance, he resumed expressing his chain of thoughts. "The one true grace of his life was the love of Héloïse. However, even this love caused conflict within him. He was a man with great confidence in reason, but found no solace in faith. He perceived not with his heart, but with his intellect. Given his propensity toward reason and rationale, he could not judge between love and lust, and, being fearful of possessing the latter, he denied himself the former. This dichotomy must have been a source of abject loneliness in him for which he expressed no remorse at being its author." Making clear his next point, the old man emphasized, "It is the subsequent death of Héloïse these years later that brings me here to weep at this graveside for the first time and reveal to you the reason you were requested to attend this unholy exhumation."

He escorted me back to the opened grave to continue his explanation, "I asked you here to face something greater than you or I."

"Death?" I asked the old man as I peered into the deep, dark hole.

Yes," he replied, "But more than that. It is to face the finiteness of this existence. It is to understand that what is

3

done on earth by men is meaningless in the scheme of things for God's Creation, that our struggles on earth are meant to cleanse us for an existence beyond this one, and that successes by us or injustices perpetrated against us are nothing to deter us from ever looking beyond this world and into the next. I tell you this to prepare you for what I am now compelled to divulge."

Out of habit, I gave not a moment's pause before courteously rebutting the point he was trying to make. "Yet a person's story is not over with death. It is not ended until all descendants, friends, followers, and memories likewise fade away; as long as thoughts of him remain, or his ideas linger, or his works perpetuate, the story lives on. This finite life may prove nearly immortal by its effect upon the beliefs, hopes, and aspirations of generations to come even if the identity of the original inspirer has become obscure. A life abundant with love toward others is emblematic of the infinite. Death cannot conquer love. The grave cannot contain it."

Our friendly debate was interrupted by the diggers' spades ringing out a singular sound as they got close to the lid of the vault. Each shovel-full of dirt thrown from the pit now caused my heart to jump when it landed with a heavy pound upon one of the fresh mounds of soil near the perimeter of the grave.

Despite much personal and professional risk, the old man had rescued Abelard's body from an ignominious burial. "Bernard had hoped to dispose of Abelard quietly in life by making him abbot of the undistinguished abbey of St. Gildas," he recounted. "By Abelard's design, Héloïse would endure a similar fate at the convent of La Paracléte. Bernard would have interred Abelard at the abbey at Cluny, far away from his beloved La Paracléte where he was most revered.

Through great intercession by me, the body was handed over to Héloïse."

The old man continued, "Héloïse pleaded with me that his body be stealthily brought to this cemetery. Then, on her deathbed, she made me vow to 'lay her by her love.' Knowing that no woman could be buried in an abbey's graveyard, it is obvious that she planned a score of years ago for this day."

While the dirt was being scraped off the stone atop the vault, the old man and I readied Héloïse's body for lowering into the grave. We reverently removed the plain woollen shroud in which her body had been wrapped for transportation to this place and exposed a lavish blue garment and a face, though now aged and lifeless, of unsurpassed beauty. Such a countenance elicited a tear from my eye that dropped upon her ashen cheek.

Perhaps there was divine reconciliation. It was unusual for an ordinary man to have such a vault. Often even the lesser nobles of the king's court spent eternity in a coffin alone. But this was all part of her plan. With enormous effort, two of the fossoyeurs started to raise the lid of the vault; and with everyone's assistance, it was propped up against the side of the grave to reveal the tapestry pall Héloïse had fashioned for placement upon the coffin. As the wooden top of the coffin was levered loose and slightly cracked open, a strong scent of bodily humours flooded the pit. Work was halted long enough for the men to tie cloths around their nose and mouth. Then, after they resumed their effort, and began removing the casket lid, in a sudden motion the ethereal, emaciated arms of Abelard reached out.

"God help us!" cried one of the gravediggers as he scrambled out of the hole.

5

"He's coming to get us!" another asserted as he, too, hurriedly climbed out of the grave.

Gathered around the edge of the site, everyone seemed frozen in place by either fright or morbid curiosity, except for the old man who presented a calming and respectful observation. "Do you not see?" he began with tears welling up in his eyes, "It is as if those arms are held forth to embrace his descending Héloïse."

In mute comportment the workmen gently lowered Héloïse's body into the coffin alongside her beloved Abelard. She had made previous arrangements for the coffin to be oversized in order to accommodate the two corpses. I left the workers to finish their task, but, also, to find the old man who had wandered away from the scene. I discovered him in the shadow of Abelard's marker. He put his arm across my shoulders and offered a verbal epitaph, "Resting or restless now for eternity I do not know, for each was loved, but failed to requite love. May God have mercy on their souls."

After compensating the labourers and dismissing the others in attendance, the old man took hold of my arm to steady himself, not so much out of physical feebleness, but because he was still shaken by recent events. "You are right," the old man admitted as he recalled an earlier statement I had made, "The story has not ended, but it is indeed in the final chapter. Indulge me to start at the beginning while the fossoyeurs finish and I will explain the circumstances that brought us to this gruesome place."

He led me on a winding trip around the gravestones to the cemetery's edge and into the modest convent. "I was a witness throughout most of Abelard's adult life," the old man stated as we trod the cobblestone pathway through the dark garden together. "I watched as his life evolved into unfortunate proportions and I studied it as a great lesson of life which I must impart to you. But a lesson hard-learned by someone should not be casually offered to the benefit of another. Instead, it should be doled out in ratio to the effort expended in understanding it. Uncover the truth in these lessons by hearing the outcome of those who suffered their teachings."

We headed down a narrow hallway that took us past the convent's chapel and to a room reserved for visiting clergy. I followed his lead through the door of this austere and private room where he had recently spent time prior to Héloïse's demise. Down on the rough-hewn plank table in the centre of the room he flung a leather satchel he had been carrying over his shoulder all evening as if its weight was a yoke he chose to bear. He reached inside this worn and dusty baggage to produce a manuscript and explained, "Into my hands was entrusted what Abelard expected to be his most lasting work. It is his biography written in Latin by his own hand and entitled '*Historia Calamitatum*', meaning '*The Story of My Misfortunes*'. For the past twenty years I have kept it from the grasp of his enemies who would seek nothing more but to destroy it. I have shared it with no one, until this time, when I want you to have it." He slid the manuscript across the table and motioned for me to sit as he continued his speech, "Listen upon the story that is the basis of this work, upon verbal footnotes Abelard related to me during its composition, and upon details of which I alone have privy knowledge."

He shuffled around the room to get a bottle of wine and two goblets from a primitive cupboard that stored little else, and then stoked the dying embers in the fireplace before finally settling into a chair across the table from me. Peering into my eyes and holding my gaze for a moment, the old man warned, "May you find pity for the previous bearer of this work as I have for the new possessor of it, for your life will never be the same once the telling of this tale is o'er."

Chapter One

An Imprisoned Soul

*T*he seed the gardener has sown is grown and ripened.

The abbey of St. Gildas de Rhuys was neither a joyous nor a holy place. Even though word about the residents' immorality had preceded my sojourn there, the sinister atmosphere of the place surpassed my suspicions. And, while I was experiencing uncomfortable feelings here, as one who could freely leave, I knew the place undoubtedly troubled the soul of the captive I came to visit.

This site had become a waste-ground for our profession. To dispose of an unruly or disobedient monk was to send him to St. Gildas. If rumours were true, drunkenness, misuse of Church funds, whoring, gluttony, and sloth ran rampant at this abbey. From the looks of the untended gardens, the profusion of garbage and human excrement around the grounds, plus the overall filth of the monks, there was irrefutable evidence of the latter deadly sin.

My uneasiness was not relieved by subsequent discourse with members of the abbey. Their cool, sanctimonious and sectarian manner was unbecoming to brethren responding to one of their own. If I was not to be considered a fellow in their midst, no doubt, neither was their abbot.

I asked one young and less coarse-looking monk where I might find the abbot. Protocol would have been for him to escort me to his superior. Instead he mumbled and pointed directions that would send me into the main building and down a dark corridor past the great hall of the abbey. I learned that Abelard had sequestered the abbey's scriptorium as his living quarters from which he rarely ventured.

The journey to St. Gildas had taken most of the day and the monks were congregating for evening vespers. I was slightly relieved to see they could conduct themselves in some pious manner. As they entered, double-file, into the great hall they chanted,

> *"De profundis clamavi ad te, Domine;*
> *Domine, audi vocem meam!"*

Which means,

> *"From the depths I cried to you, Lord;*
> *Lord, hear my voice!"*

And, as I moved down the hallway the chanting echoed softly,

> *"Si delictorum memoriam servaveris,*
> *Domine, Domine, quis sustinebit?"*

In my head, I translated the Latin verse,

> *"If you remember only our iniquities,*
> *Lord, Lord, who can survive it?"*

I reached the end of the stone-lined passage and stopped at a heavy wooden door to listen to the last faint phrases from the monks' processional chant,

> *"Sed penes te est peccatorum venia,*
> *Ut cum reverentia serviatur tibi."*

And I sensed the appropriateness of those words,

> *"But in your hands is the forgiveness of sins, that you may be served in reverence."*

Under my breath, I joined their singing,

> *"Spero in Dominum;*
> *Sperat anima mea in verbum eius,"*

Which means,

> *"I trust in the Lord;*
> *My soul trusts in his word."*

The monks ended their chant with a glorious roundelay of "Amen" seemingly too beautiful to be coming from such a band of scoundrels. Its enchanting melody caused me to further pause in front of the abbot's portal. After what felt as aeons, I moved to look through a peephole in the massive door. The large chamber beyond this obstruction appeared dark and lifeless until I caught a glimpse of a shuffling figure in the farthermost corner. Possibly aroused by the monks' musical invocation, the figure proceeded slowly across the room and was visible only at times by a flickering light that accompanied it.

The figure hesitated, and upon lighting a large candle with the small taper he had been carrying, the room became illuminated enough to recognize Pierre Abelard. This was a man in his early sixties, more than tired-looking, who showed scars from bearing ponderous worldly and spiritual burdens. He placed writing instruments on an easel and sat before it, deeply contemplating what was to be scribed upon this manuscript.

Almost as being sentenced to prison, Abelard was unexpectedly elected abbot of St. Gildas. Powerful enemies had advocated his election to this position. The appointment was not meant as a commendation for previous meritorious service or as an effort to utilize Abelard's unique abilities to reform the inhabitants of this abbey. This was a bold-faced attempt to silence him. Yet, I took some umbrage for the insignificant part I played in what had happened to him. Although not the perpetrator of his problems, not his prosecutor, or his enemy, I confess still to lingering remorse for being a bystander in the whole affair. However, in the scheme of things, my visits to him and persistent prayers for him were penitence enough for any slight wrong I may have done him.

Hearing footsteps behind me, I quickly turned around to meet a servant monk carrying a wooden bowl full of food, a small wine cask, and a goblet. Virtually shoving me aside, he pushed open the weighty door, but proceeded no further into the room.

"Master," the monk spoke, "I have brought your evening meal."

The reply from within came from someone who sounded quite exhausted, "Put it down and leave me."

The monk deposited the victuals on a table near Abelard and poured wine into the goblet. As he departed, his path once more crossed mine, and he sent an icy glare of disapproval toward me for no other reason, I suppose, than my presence there. He had left the door wide open, completely exposing me to Abelard who either did not notice or acknowledge my attendance. Just before I uttered my first word to him, Abelard began to recite from the Book of John, chapter 15, verses 18-19,

> *"If the world hates you, ye know that it hated me before it hated you."*

And from verse 20,

> *"If they have persecuted me, they will persecute you."*

He thumbed through marked pages of a huge Bible on a stand next to him. He would pause to read several verses, often mouthing the words; while certain passages, which obviously aroused deeper passion in him, he read aloud. "Galatians 1, verse 10," began Abelard, "I do not seek to please men, for if I pleased men, I should not be the servant of God." Then prayerfully he added, "I give thanks to God that I am worthy to be one whom the world despises." He closed the Bible and returned to the easel.

I took this as an opportunity to make myself known to him. The best I could muster was a sheepish knock on the already opened door. Not even looking up, Abelard made retort for this interruption, "I said leave me, and remove that which you call sustenance from me, for I am attended by an Almighty Hand through which I am sustained."

"Friend," I said softly.

"Friend?" asked Abelard. "Who is it that assumes such an undistinguished honour?"

Stepping forward I replied, "It is I, old friend, Alberic."

"Fidus Achates!" With more energy Abelard rose from his stool and met me halfway across the room. He clutched both my arms and gently shook them while he asked, "Tell me, how is my garden?"

Trying to reassure him, I answered truthfully, "Your garden is healthy and green. The seed the gardener has sown is grown and ripened." Upon this statement, a rare moment of contentment came over him and he smiled at me.

It had been several years since last I saw Abelard, not since he had become abbot of this objectionable place, but it seemed like a lifetime when I assessed the toll his forced residency had taken on him. Almost everything about him had changed. Physically, he no longer moved with strength and vigour, but with arched back and bowed shoulders. Mental fatigue was apparent, and the fire in his eyes was dim. Yet, he remained steadfastly concerned for the garden of which he never failed to ask me.

Abelard went deliberately to the door. He closed it and locked it with the bolt. He then turned back to me in anguish and cried, "Has Satan beset me to such an extent that I no longer know where I may find rest? I am driven wither and yon, a fugitive and a vagabond. The violence of my enemies I see if I leave the cloister, but …within… I must endure the crafty machinations of those monks who are called my sons and who are entrusted to me as their father."

Abelard was now at the table. He snatched the bowl of food and dashed it to the floor. "Oh, how often they have tried to kill me with poison! I must safeguard myself from their daily plotting lest it be deemed I am a rash tempter of God rather than a lover of Him." He grabbed a knife from the table and continued the tirade, "Nay, lest it be judged that I had taken my own life."

It seemed like this last possibility quieted him. He returned the knife to the table and lifted the goblet of wine. I began to believe the strain upon his mind, because of his exile to this place, had been far greater than I first imagined. He was deluded, I thought. Some evil had befallen him, and, yes, his life's work had been condemned, but to believe that his peers would have premeditatedly sent him to an ignominious death at St. Gildas was inconceivable to me.

He offered me the goblet, which I took, and spoke in a hushed voice, "They have sought to destroy me in the very ceremony of the altar by putting poison in the chalice." I peered deeply into the dark, blood red wine and replaced the goblet on the table without drinking from it.

Abelard smiled slightly. Perhaps this was because he believed he had converted me to his way of thinking and gained a sympathizer to his plight. More likely though, he smiled because I was too weak to try my own convictions by tasting the wine he had challenged me to drink.

Composed now, Abelard pointed out, "We should endure our persecutions all the more steadfastly the more bitterly they harm us. Rightfully do all men say, 'Thy will be done.'"

As if I was no longer present, Abelard sat once more at the easel, took pen in hand, and began writing with unsteady strokes. After a while, he read aloud what had just been written:

> *"I, Pierre Abelard, know that, often, the hearts of men and of women are stirred, as likewise they are soothed in their sorrows, more by example than by*

words. Therefore, because I, too, have known some consolation from speech with one who has suffered as I, am I commissioned to write of the sufferings which have sprung out of my misfortunes; of the one who, though absent, is of herself ever a consoler; and of Him, my comfort still."

The vesper bell tolled nine, signalling the end of the evening's vigilance. I felt somehow compelled to remain with Abelard throughout the night while he laboured on his manuscript.

Chapter Two

The Privileged Life

I *fled from the court of Mars that I might win learning in the bosom of Minerva.*

Everything had come easily to Abelard. His home-life had been conducive to intellectual development. Above that was his own innate ability to make what was difficult for others simple to him. It is hard to understand how a man could live such an ideal life during his formative years, without conflict or challenge, and still mature with any depth of character. I always felt that to achieve success in this world one must first face failure, for the manner in which one handles failure is what leads to success. Just as there can be no courage without fear, joy without sadness, abundance without poverty, or good without evil, neither can success exist without failure. Abelard's life contradicted this axiom. He never failed in what he set out to do. Success bred success until, ultimately, too much success led to his failure.

According to his own description of his early life, Abelard came from a small town called Le Pallet, which was situated on the way to Lesser Brittany, south of the Loire River, a distance of eight miles from the city of Nantes. He said that minds that bend easily to the study of letters was the nature of those who dwelled in that country. He was born in the year 1079, the son of a knight. His father, however, had a smattering of letters before he girded on the soldier's belt. And so it happened, according to Abelard's account, that his father's love of letters, being so strong, he saw to it that each son of his should be taught in letters even earlier than in the management of arms. Therefore, Abelard being his first-born, and for that reason especially dear to him, he sought with double diligence to have him wisely taught.

Abelard often spoke about his father's own sagacity. When lecturing, Abelard would sometimes use a phrase or a story that he remembered from his days of youth when his father profusely dispensed wisdom upon the family. In dramatic fashion, his father would tell tales of warfare, blood, and glory that held Abelard and his younger brothers spellbound and kept his mother and sisters squeamish as they tried not to pay heed to the knight's gory details. But at the end of each tale, he would try to add something philosophical such as, "A warrior who faces death at every turn of battle quickly understands how precious life is, and in service to others how it is also a privilege." According to Abelard, one of his most oft-repeated points was, "No one should take the privilege of living for granted, whatever their station, or squander it by not adhering to the calling of one's heart. Life is not just a gift from God, but life has been entrusted to us by God so that we may fulfil His purposes." Of course, we all knew that life is more complex than that, but we, fellow students and scholastics, listened respectfully when Abelard felt a need to impart this paternal acumen to us.

Early on, Abelard challenged his masters and criticized their teachings. He was never content to accept what was being taught him without debate or cross-examination. These masters felt that Abelard was displaying contempt toward them and their views, and soon arguments concerning philosophical issues were replaced with personal conflicts between teacher and student.

Conflicts never deterred him from his quest for knowledge however, and the more Abelard went forward in his studies, the greater became his devotion to them. This devotion grew to a point where he said that he gladly left to his brothers the pomp and glory in arms, the right of heritage, and all the honours that should have been his as the eldest. He once said to me, "I fled from the court of Mars that I might win learning in the bosom of Minerva." He believed that the armoury of logical reasoning was more powerful than any arsenal of man-made weaponry – beyond which, he could clearly see destiny beckoning to him, and he restlessly wanted to see where it might lead him.

So, with the full blessing of a loving father, Abelard did set out into a new world, not knowing what to expect, nor did the world know what to expect from him.

Chapter Three

Deliverance

*W*hat life may come of this, we do not know.

It was as if I already knew her. Our lives in many ways ran parallel, and information about her was eagerly gathered by my empathetic ear because of several experiences I sensed we had in common.

I have come to feel that to know a person well is to know their past well. The deeper one probes into another's past, the greater is one's understanding of the other. The influences, the achievements, even the tragedies of past generations sift down to shape the present personality. A great desire to understand another exhibits a depth of caring for that person. Understanding takes time and patience. It is the slow process of refining the true metal of a person or discovering what may be only a wash across their surface. It is a melting in life's crucible of two until a precious ore is coined between them.

This concept is nothing new and I do not consider myself profound by the postulating of it. But, in a society that is opening its floodgates to new ideas, has new and acquirable materialistic possessions in profusion, and is often concerned with only the facile, apparent and obvious, I am compelled to restate the importance of effort, time, and perseverance in fostering understanding. It leads to a virtuous life. True to the essence of what I am saying, let me engage you in some background history surrounding those whose lives this story revolves. There have been two whom I have studied most diligently.

Héloïse was the niece of Canon Fulbert, one of the most prominent men at the Cathedral School of Paris. Out of deep respect, I must first mention his credentials. Fulbert was one of Europe's greatest schoolmasters. He directly descended from a crop of superior students taught by one of the greatest schoolmasters of all time, Gerbert of Aurillac. Fulbert could be a great storyteller when he wanted to be and if the subject suited him. But, forever the teacher, his stories were always designed to impart volumes of knowledge and information. A favourite subject was the lineage of learning from Aristotle to the present. And, since I was obliged to hear it repeated many times by him over the years, I hope you will constrain any impatience at allowing me to pass this information on to you this once.

History will remember Gerbert best as Pope Sylvester II. By virtue of his renowned teaching skills he secured papal election with the assistance of his friend, Otto III, emperor of the Holy Roman Empire. It was the year 999. Many of the new Pope's contemporaries believed that the end of the millennium would usher in the victorious return of Christ and, so, they became complacent while waiting for His arrival. Not so with Gerbert who used his high position with zeal to establish the Church in Hungary and to found new centres of learning throughout Europe. He was the first French pope, and unfortunately for us all, his tenure was only a short four years.

Gerbert had been born in Auvergne, the son of a serf. Had it not been for the far-sighted vision and reign of the great philosopher-king, Charlemagne, almost two hundred years earlier, Gerbert may have died a serf. Charlemagne knew that education was the vital spark needed to ignite the world and dispel those dark times. He engendered scholarship, decreeing that every monastery should provide a school to teach all those "who with God's help are able to learn."

The king's hopes for increased educational opportunities were realized nowhere better than in France. Monastery schools, which were designed originally to perpetuate their own order, soon found themselves in competition with cathedral schools. These cathedral schools taught candidates for the secular clergy, that is, those who would serve the needs of the common public rather than the "needs" of God and the organized Church. Since serving man was considered less noble than serving God, at first, the monastery schools were held in the highest regard and attracted the most talented and well-bred of candidates. The cathedral schools, on the other hand, became meshed with the everyday life of the growing towns to such an extent that they became accessible to laymen. As the number of cathedral schools increased, more and more students were recruited from the burgeoning class of merchants that had arisen from the flourishing trade associated with the new town society. Soon, even talented serfs were allowed admission into these schools.

The curriculum of these cathedral schools consisted of the seven liberal arts, so named because in ancient Rome, their study was the exclusive right of the *liberi*, or free men. Now, it was the renewed study of these liberal arts that was beginning to make men free once more and causing the dawn of a new age. Texts, however, were from the manuscripts of our early Church Fathers, such as St. Augustine, who were known as *auctores*, that is, authorities, whose words religious leaders, let alone students, would not presume to challenge or contradict.

Gerbert was a candidate of such a cathedral school at the abbey of St. Gerard. Quickly his natural brilliance shone amongst the students, impressing the abbot to such an extent that he was offered the distinctive opportunity to study mathematics at Catalonia in northern Spain. Two centuries prior to this time, Spain had been invaded by a Muslim people called the Moors and was still being ruled by them when Gerbert left for Catalonia.

Upon his arrival, Gerbert was greeted by local students and nobility as eager to learn from him as he was eager to learn from them. This intellectual love affair between Gerbert and the Moors lasted for several years during which time he travelled extensively. In the course of one excursion into southern Spain, he visited the city of Cordova on the Guadaliquiver River. There he was struck in awe at a centre of learning that alone could accommodate thousands of students. He had never before seen such extensive educational systems as those established by this Arab and Berber people whose intellectual society had an ancient link with Alexandria, a centre for learning of mythological proportions. Alexandria's fabled harbour lighthouse epitomized the city's role as the light of the ancient world, and its intellectual fire remained burning in the minds of its distant descendants in Cordova. While there, Gerbert was able to peruse copies of rescued manuscripts long presumed lost with the destruction of Alexandria's legendary 500,000 volume library to gain insights not afforded most European scholastics of his time.

An even more important and lasting impression upon Gerbert, however, was the effect the Moor's tolerant culture had on him. He acquired the questioning, questing spirit of his Moorish counterparts that allowed for personal freethinking and open-mindedness toward other people's thoughts and beliefs. With such a disposition, he returned to France.

Being only shortly a student there, the cathedral school at Rheims made Gerbert the schoolmaster. This paved the way for an educational upheaval of such proportions that we still feel its ripples today. He announced that the works of the auctores were insufficient and his pupils were, henceforth, to study the Greek classics of Aristotle and the Roman works of Porphyry and Cicero in the original.

Perhaps his greatest accomplishment was to give new life to the quadrivium, which is the higher division of the liberal arts consisting of arithmetic, geometry, astronomy, and music, by rescuing it from its textbook decadence and injecting it with real and practical interpretations. He replaced the cumbersome Roman numeral system with the Arabic numerals 1–9, employed a simplified abacus and instructed his pupils on its use, and taught astronomy by means of a model showing the movements of the planets.

It was in this enlightened and fresh atmosphere where Fulbert's intellect breathed. Under the tutorage of disciples of Gerbert, he became proficient in the art of dialectics. This is the practice of examining opinions or ideas by the method of question and answer to test their validity. This was the root of his own open-minded nature and he held no issue too sacred for argument as long as the debate aided the advancement of human understanding, for he would not abide trivialities.

The rest of Fulbert's past is sketchy, for even though he was a fountain of information otherwise, he was reluctant to speak of himself. Now, Fulbert was not a shy man, neither was he egocentric. He had been able to arrest himself from the almost inevitable sense of self-importance associated with his position. I believe he considered it a weakness to rest on past laurels or dwell upon personal accomplishments. He was the most forward-looking man I ever knew.

From other sources, I learned that Fulbert had been born of a moderately wealthy family. At around the age of fourteen, when young men of his status should be taking up training in arms, he developed a chronic illness that left him weak and fatigued. Useless as a soldier, his mother introduced him to the study of letters as a diversion from the sting of being unable to carry out his manly obligations. Little did she know then how immense a gift she had bestowed upon her son and upon the rest of us.

Later in life, as he pursued his education, shunning the monastery schools which might have fostered sooner entry into the hierarchy of Church politics, Fulbert's thirst for knowledge led him to the highly respected cathedral school of Rheims that had been re-established under Gerbert's supervision. From student, to lecturer, to schoolmaster, Fulbert was well received by all. His nonabrasive nature and tolerance toward others less profound than he, won him great popularity. He later became Bishop of Chartes and was the driving force of its cathedral school.

Fulbert did more than fill his pupils' heads with information. His genius inspired within them a zest for dialectics, and he compelled them to express their ideas in their own words. Then, almost in retirement because of poor health, he brought that same predilection for openness to the cathedral school at Paris where I met him.

Under a reduced workload, Fulbert taught whom he wanted and where he wanted. Both Abelard and I were fortunate enough to be part of the inner circle of followers attending the lectures he held informally throughout Paris. As had become the custom, classrooms were not delineated by ponderous, confining walls, but had become any airy or familiar place chosen by the master. Fulbert might have us meet at the banks of the Seine on a sunny summer day, or at his home during winter months where we would sit on straw strewn upon the floor to insulate us from the cold and damp stone.

This relaxed structure of education brought about fierce competition between cathedral schools in acquiring the most popular teachers. Since facilities meant nothing, entire universities could pick up and leave a city at the whim of an influential schoolmaster. Students were most loyal to their masters, even above self, as I was to Fulbert.

But I have digressed enough. Earlier, I mentioned that I felt as if I knew Héloïse even before I met her. Fulbert had spoken of her often and enthusiastically. I learned from him that she had been pathetically orphaned even before birth. Fulbert's younger brother and only sibling, Albertus, was Héloïse's father. Having the same noble blood surging through his heart as his older brother, Albertus also felt similar urgings to make a mark in the world, but his attempt was manifest in quite a different way than Fulbert's.

Albertus was the image of his father, Hugo, who was the founder and absolute head of their modest, yet comfortable, household. Having faithfully served two of the Capetian royal families, Hugo had been granted a parcel of wilderness in northern France and enough gold to prudently turn the land into a self-sufficient society under his control. Before leaving the service of the King, Hugo had met, and ardently desired, a woman of the lower nobility. She was of only average appearance but of great intelligence and of equally great heart. She had been betrothed to a nobleman who met a sudden, untimely death from an undetermined illness - some accounts intimate that he had not succumbed to a natural affliction. Nonetheless, this was a fortunate event for Hugo and his progeny, for he successfully managed to win the hand of this lady who was so grief-stricken over the loss of her beloved that she cared not much about what else might befall her. Not of small significance, too, was the fact that the wealth and generosity of her family contributed much to the early success of Hugo's estate.

Hugo and his wife ended up struggling happily together during the first years of their marriage with their two young sons. However, Hugo's insatiable appetite to possess more land, wealth, and power soon began to cause turmoil among the family. For a while, the mother's pacifying influence tempered the effects of his aggressive, dictatorial attitude, but Hugo's domination became almost complete. He demanded, and received, loyalty bordering on utter devotion to himself and to his dominion. This was true of all his family, friends, and feudal servants, except perhaps for one, Fulbert.

Both Hugo and his youngest son, Albertus, were robust men of their day. Neither did anything in moderation. They could consume their share of food and wine, out fight the strongest, outwit the shrewdest, and become the most impassioned when some cause deserved their righteous indignation. There were driving hungers they needed to satisfy. It was commonly known that for several years Hugo had maintained a mistress who resided in an obscure village in the wilderness not far from his estate. It was hinted to me, by Fulbert, that she bore him a daughter who was, years later, frequented by Hugo's son.

When Albertus had reached the proper age, he travelled to Paris for an extended trip. Upon his return, he brought with him a bride from the same family as his mother's. Thus, he had firmly established himself, and, barring any rights of primogeniture, he was his father's favourite and expected heir.

Fulbert was not especially upset by his apparent disinheritance for he had always planned to leave the confines of his home to explore the vast regions of knowledge calling him to come. His mother adored him for his profound intelligence and charismatic personality, and her maternal encouragement enthused confidence within him. Hugo noted his wife's doting on her special son and offered financial assistance for him to seek further education as a means to prod his departure. From that point on, Fulbert rarely returned home and, if he did, only for brief visits. Nonetheless, Fulbert's mother and sister-in-law, who were devout Christians, anxiously anticipated those visits to hear of his experiences and to laud his success in attaining status in the Church's hierarchy. Their praise of Fulbert landed hard upon their husbands' ears, and the two men began to take offence at its repetition.

Still feeling in competition with the repute of his absent brother, and with an affected display of pious fervour, Albertus announced he was going to join the crusading army that was leaving to wrest the Holy City from the hands of the Saracens. "To serve God with a strong right arm is the noblest thing a man can do," were the words he spoke from atop horseback as he prepared to depart from his father, mother, and wife.

"*In hoc signo vinces*," his mother recited Great Constantine's motto, *IHS*, "*in this sign you will conquer*," and she presented him a tunic emblazoned with a red cross patee. She privately recalled having recited the same slogan to another son at his departure from home.

As with all such foolish young men, the idea of meeting with misadventure in battle never crossed his mind. Yet, in the very first conflict an enemy archer pierced Albertus' gorget with his arrow, inflicting a mortal wound. Pithed by the sharp point lodged in the back of his neck, Albertus laid motionless on the bloody battlefield for almost two days while the stench of rotting flesh from the fallen soldiers all around him became almost smothering. A passing squire, thinking Albertus a casualty, had rolled him prone on his back and crossed his arms over his chest to cradle his long sword. In motionless, yet conscious vigilance he waited on death with only his innermost thoughts for solace or torment.

This occurred in the year 1098. I remember this because it was the year of my birth. Fulbert told me that Albertus' wife, who was much younger than her husband, was unknowingly pregnant for the first time when her husband left on his religious adventure. While she was in labour, news arrived of Albertus' death. Family and friends intercepted the message and decided not to disclose the dreadful information until a more fitting time. Héloïse's mother sensed the discomfort caused by the painful news in those present for the childbirth. She pried loose the hidden knowledge from one of the midwives. It will never be known for certain whether it was the hard birthing or abject grief that caused her demise, but she lay dead on her bloodied bed with the child yet unborn.

The physician in attendance took deep sympathy on the woeful turn of events. "What life may come of this, we do not know," he pronounced as he dismissed the others in attendance. "Even great Caesar had a flawed beginning," he said quietly to Hugo, the last one still lingering in the room.

Understanding what the physician was offering, "If it was to be the son of my lost son, hurry, I pray thee, for his resurrection," petitioned Hugo. "I shall not ever mention, nor will I ever forget, the miracle I ask."

In privacy, the physician conducted the ancient operation known for centuries but now forbidden to perform under penalty of death. Had it not been for this courageous and caring act, the life of Héloïse, too, would have been forfeited.

Héloïse's early life proved not much easier than its beginning. Of course, Hugo was distraught that she had not been a grandson. Before Héloïse was old enough to recognize either his good or bad qualities, her grandfather was reportedly killed by an errant arrow in a hunting accident. Perhaps this was just as well, for Hugo never regained his zest for living after the death of Albertus. In fact, life under him had become harsh. Hugo no longer tended his property carefully. Instead he bled his assets dry for personal indulgence. He purchased the most costly wines and horses, and became involved with gambling and indecent women to alleviate his grief. All but the barest essentials he denied his wife and Héloïse.

Hugo sank to his lowest level of humanity one evening after consuming too much of his expensive wine. In a drunken stupor, he rode off toward a village in the woods and there raped and strangled to death a young peasant mother. Due to his high social ranking the incident was virtually ignored by the officials. Rumours were, however, that judgment was executed swiftly by an avenging arrow loosed by the woman's lover when he returned from afar and discovered what had taken place.

Upon Hugo's death, as matriarchal head of the family, Héloïse's grandmother saw to the preservation of the property. More importantly, she provided early intellectual guidance for Héloïse.

From an early age, it was obvious that Héloïse had inherited the noble character of her mother and grandmother. If ever there was evidence that blood ran bluer in some people's veins than others, Héloïse provided such evidence. Yet a child, she would go to the fields with her grandmother to give the labourers their orders. She did not shrink from their protestations if they disliked their tasks and she, with grandmother at her side, would stand firm against the coarsest of looks and language.

Héloïse's grandmother told her many stories about life under Capetian rule. She showed her the beautiful garments she once wore as a lady of the king's court and filled Héloïse's head with fancy about chivalrous suitor knights. Héloïse would mimic her grandmother's regal bearing of straight stature and uplifted head while playing in some of those lavish gowns that would have required years for her to grow into.

At the tender age of seven, just old enough for Héloïse to begin understanding the events of one's life, her grandmother became ill. In her weakened state the fiefdom began to collapse. The serfs became independent and lazy. For the reasons of reduced productivity and Hugo's squandering of the reserves, the once heritable land became hopelessly debt-ridden.

Fulbert had neither extended any assistance nor even contacted his mother during those years. Unexpectedly, the property was overtaken by an adjoining landholder. Héloïse and her grandmother were whisked away to a nearby nunnery. I must assume that Fulbert, being the sole remaining male member of the family, and, as such, holding absolute right, did negotiate some monetary transaction for the property and arranged for the care of his niece and mother.

Very soon after her relocation, Héloïse's grandmother grew drastically worse in health. Héloïse confided to me years later that, while she was at her grandmother's deathbed, she overheard her speak to her confessor these words, "Only the agony felt at the loss of my husband equals the agony felt at the loss of his life's work. He hoped that the land he so laboriously tended would be passed down from generation to generation. As long as the land remained, he was eternal and I was with him. Now it is gone and I have lost my husband once more."

This pathos must have been a contributing factor to her accelerated passing away. Like her daughter-in-law, she would be reunited to her most beloved through a death that had been hastened by grief.

With her grandmother's passing, the nuns took over the care of Héloïse, but they provided only the most basic needs of food, clothing, and shelter. Still only a child, they bothered little to nourish her spirit. As she grew, the nuns added menial tasks to her routine, which she completed without spite and in a cheerful manner. Eventually, the abbess sensed a strength of character and exceptional intelligence in the young maiden. She also noticed the blossoming of great feminine beauty and a charismatic allure about Héloïse that far surpassed the average candidate for the nunnery. She interceded on behalf of Héloïse through correspondence with Fulbert to obtain special privileges and circumstances for his niece. He conceded.

Fulbert's influential position in the Church's political system gave Héloïse unequalled opportunities for education as a girl. First, she became proficient in the trivium, which is the three lower liberal arts consisting of grammar, logic, and rhetoric. Then, at fifteen years of age, because of her previously demonstrated abilities, she was allowed to study the quadrivium at one of the smaller cathedral schools.

As I mentioned earlier, the coincidences of our lives were startling. Like Héloïse, I never knew a father or mother. My grandmother cared for me and we struggled financially. One day I found myself in a monastery, and later, at the university in Paris, learning about things I never expected my mind to entertain. Some miracle had brought me this far. Soon some miracle was going to do the same for her.

All of Héloïse's actions had been carefully monitored by her uncle who understood the possible ramifications of this unique experiment. She had just turned seventeen when Fulbert summoned her to Paris.

Chapter Four

Triumphal Entry

*O*h, *Paris, steal Helen away again!*

It would have been a glorious day for Héloïse. She must have felt chills of excitement when she saw for the first time the outline of Paris on the horizon at her approach. I know how awe inspiring it was when I first set eyes on the city. She and her companion, Thessaly, had an exhilarating trip over the past few days. The early spring weather had been delightful. There was the accompanying aroma of wild flowers and lush green growth as they travelled by horse-drawn cart down paths kept slightly muddy by mid-morning showers. Young birds were chirping from their nests in the budding trees. Rabbits, squirrels, quail, and pheasants were out with their broods and litters absorbing the sun's generous warmth. A hart with his fallow doe and newborn fawn grazed freely upon a grassy hill. There was new life all around Héloïse. Who would not be affected by its wonder?

The alabastrine island city of Paris sat in the middle of the river known by the ancient world as the 'Sequana'. On the island were all the important institutions of the region, the king's palace, the royal abbey, the University of Paris, and the marketplace. Along with royalty, clergy, and scholastics, wealthy merchants and tradesmen had also recently gained the privilege of inhabiting this precious ground. Long spans of the original wall that once followed the whole perimeter of the city along the edge of the river still existed, not so much any more for protection against invaders from without, but as if to contain all the greatness within.

After crossing the expansive bridge that led to the inner city, and upon entering through its ancient gates, the driver deposited the women's belongings alongside the street and departed. Ignoring her companion's insistence, Héloïse would not make straight for her final destination. She tarried in the streets to take in all the sights. She dallied in the marketplace to strike up conversations with strangers and merchants. For a while, Thessaly had completely lost track of Héloïse among the throng of which she seemed so eager to become a part. Thessaly was anchored by their baggage and hesitated to take chase after Héloïse for fear their belongings would be gone upon her return. Not long, however, the crowd almost seemed to spontaneously divide to allow Héloïse passage back to Thessaly's side. It was similar to the parting of the sea so she might cross into the Promised Land.

"This is an extraordinary place," she exclaimed, "I love its vibrancy which resounds in me. Oh, Paris, steal Helen away again!"

After strenuous coaxing, Thessaly finally managed to steer Héloïse's attention to the matter at hand. "We must get to your uncle's house soon. He will be expecting us and will be concerned if we are much later in our arrival." With that, Héloïse picked up her bags, and after inquiring directions, the two headed directly for the university.

"It is a wonderful feeling to be somewhere you belong," said Héloïse thinking aloud.

"Yes," sided Thessaly, "It must have been difficult being an orphan."

Worried a little about what she had just said, Héloïse explained further, "Not that the sisters weren't good to me. I appreciated all that they did. I was surrounded by love in that sisterhood, but," she added, "It will mean so much more to be with someone who is kindred."

"Is he the last of your family?" asked Thessaly.

"Yes, as far as I know, he is all that is left." Then, thinking aloud, she asked herself, "I wonder what sort of a man he is?"

Thessaly was taken aback by the question. "You mean that you have never met him? During all these years he never visited you?" she quizzed her companion.

Héloïse responded seemingly unhurt and making no apologies for her uncle's behaviour, "I have heard that he is a greatly esteemed and reverent canon of the cathedral school, an erudite and perceptive man. I know that his devotion to me is secondary to his service to God. I shall not be jealous of his times of prayer and meditation, teaching and learning, nor interfere with his destiny and legacy."

"You have not set sight on him then?" queried Thessaly who meant to sate her curiosity.

"What I have heard is not very flattering," continued Héloïse. "I hear he is short and slender in stature, has a pointed nose, and dark beady eyes."

"Sounds more the likes of a ferret to me," Thessaly quipped.

"And under his hat are two horns, and he walks with a limp because of a wooden leg," teased Héloïse in return.

"Now, I do not believe you!" Thessaly interposed, and the two laughed at each other for a while as they continued walking.

"I confess, I have not a clue as to my uncle's appearance, and I am more anxious than you to find out," said Héloïse in a more sombre way. "Though, I envision him as a great man of wisdom, and of faith that draws him near to God, and of compassion that endears him to man. Of these traits I am sure. Of the physical, I know or care not."

Being redirected by a passer-by to the exact location of Fulbert's house, the two found themselves at last standing in front of the canon's door. It was an unspectacular abode. "It is a modest dwelling, is it not, Thessaly?" observed Héloïse.

"Fulbert is a modest man with modest ways," Thessaly assured her in order to try to relieve the disappointment she sensed in her friend. "You know, it is a great privilege to live on university grounds. Only the most respected are allotted such quarters."

Héloïse was not disappointed. Things were merely not as she expected. Therein lies a difference. It was not in her nature to be disappointed of anything in her life. However, more and more often, I think life was not always as she expected.

"Knock on the door," she directed Thessaly.

After her gentle rapping, it did not take long for a servant monk to crack open the door. "Yes?" he asked dryly.

"We have come to see Fulbert," Héloïse explained.

"The good master is not here," he replied pointedly as he started to close the door.

Quickly trying to prevent its closure, Héloïse raised her voice, "Hold the door. I am his niece, Héloïse, and this is my friend, Thessaly."

The monk acknowledged his introduction to Thessaly with a nod and a word, "Sister." He then turned his attention to Héloïse. "I do not recall Canon Fulbert ever speaking of you. I had always supposed he was without family since he never spoke of any kinsmen."

"Surely he would not disclaim to have had a mother," Héloïse jested. "Even our beloved Christ had a mother, Notre Dame. Fulbert's mother was mother to me, as His is mother to us all." Trying to end this conversation, Héloïse insisted, "The simple truth is, faithful servant, that Canon Fulbert summoned me here. I am to stay a while in his house. Please let us in."

"Dear Lord," complained the monk, "I have not been instructed about this business." Then, resigning to the possibility, he added, "Since you are both virtuous women, I will take you at your word. Come in." He opened wide the door.

"Merci," the two said, as they hauled in what seemed to the monk to be a profusion of belongings.

"For two women pledged to the simple life, you seem to have an abundance of worldly possessions," observed the monk. "Material things are poison to the soul," he pointed out.

Thessaly, in their defence, responded, "Most of these are righteous possessions. Some are manuscripts we bring to Fulbert, our crucifix and rosaries, religious habiliments . . . "

Ending the excuses, "We are planning a long stay," said Héloïse.

"I hope that Fulbert is expecting the same," replied the monk still feeling put out by the women's imposition upon his domestic routine. "I suppose it was a long journey and the two of you are probably famished." He saw their eyes respond in the affirmative. "All right, I will prepare some food for you." As he headed for another room, he mumbled, "I wish he would tell me when to expect visitors. How am I to know when to prepare bedding or fetch and cook more food?" Then, looking back, he added, "And women no less!"

"I hope we did not upset the man," ventured Thessaly sardonically.

"Here, help me undress and change before my uncle comes home. I want to make a favourable impression."

"Yes, and you will feel much better in fresh garments," said Thessaly as she began tending to Héloïse's needs.

"I have something, dear Thessaly..." started Héloïse as she disposed of her outer tunic, "...That I want to show you." She pulled from one of her bags an indigo bliaut, the latest dress for fashionable ladies, with full draped skirt and belled sleeves.

"Where did you acquire that?" asked the astonished companion.

"I purchased it from one of the merchants when we came into town."

"How?" wondered Thessaly, still in shock.

"I bought it with the money Uncle Fulbert sent for travelling expenses."

"Then with what did you pay the boatman and cart driver?" interrogated Thessaly who was trying to shed further light upon Héloïse's tale.

Héloïse answered coyly, "Was not the blessing to journey in the company of a nun enough?"

In an admonishing tone, all Thessaly could say was, "Héloïse!"

Holding the dress up in front of her, Héloïse prompted her friend for a genuine opinion, "Well, truly, do you not like it?"

Shaking her head, "It is so . . . so blue!" was Thessaly's first response.

Héloïse almost laughed at the comment, but pursued in her euphoria, "Yes, is it not wonderful! The tailor swore there is not another like it in all of Paris."

Thessaly had begun feeling the fabric of the garment, "But it is blue!"

Just then, there was a clamour at the door. The young maidens inside could discern loud conversations and words of farewell from several male voices outside. They darted behind a dressing screen in the corner of the room. "Someone's coming!" muttered a panicked Thessaly. "Hurry, I'll help you dressing."

The servant monk re-entered the room carrying two bowls of food just as Fulbert made his entrance into the house. "Good day, dear master," said the monk cordially.

Fulbert, eyeing the vessels, humorously suggested, "Stealing my food again?"

The monk was taken back, "No, sir!" he protested, "This is for your niece for whom you sent."

"Who? Héloïse? Where is she, my niece?" asked an anxious Fulbert as he examined the room for her.

Thessaly poked her head out from around the screen. Uneasy about the situation herself, she began to speak with a trembling in her voice, "Sir . . . "

"There you are!" he exclaimed while beckoning to her, "Come, come out where I can get a better look at you."

She obeyed and tried to explain, "But, sir, I am . . ."

He moved toward the frightened girl in an attempt to embrace her, "Dear niece," he said as she dodged his arms, "How good it is to see some of my family after all these years." He was nearly chasing Thessaly around the room. "How wonderful a woman looks in the raiment of God."

Afore being caught by the effusive canon, Thessaly halted in her tracks, turned to her pursuer, stood rigid in face of him, and pronounced clearly, "*I am not your niece!*" Fulbert froze in place agog at this declaration. Pointing toward the screen, the maiden continued, "Your niece is not yet fully dressed."

Fulbert eyed the screen carefully and then began self-consciously tidying himself up a bit for the reunion. "Well, I have waited seventeen years to meet my niece," Fulbert philosophized while raising an eyebrow at the first object of his chase, "I can wait a few moments longer."

"No need for you to wait another moment my dear uncle. I am ready," announced Héloïse as she stepped out from the dressing area. She kissed and embraced her uncle who was flushed with alarm at what he saw. "How I have waited for this moment!" she added.

Fulbert was disturbed. "This is my niece? Where is your habit? And why is your hair loose?" he asked in a disapproving tone.

"I am not yet vowed to God," she answered, "and this is the appropriate dress of the times for a young maiden."

Not convinced, Fulbert objected, "It is the colour of the Devil."

"Nonsense!" Héloïse refuted, "It is the colour of the sky, home of Heaven, the hue of peace and tranquillity. It is the shade of the shimmering sea, full of life and wonders."

"Monk's cloth would have been more suitable," Canon Fulbert muttered loudly enough to be understood.

"Then would you have me shave my head and bind my breasts to pass as a brother?" She asked pointedly.

Fulbert was amused. "No you are too beautiful," he responded, "They would find you out." This time, he embraced her warmly. He then held her at arm's length for closer inspection. "You have the looks of my brother," he observed, "Flaxen hair with streaks of sunlight, eyes that catch the light and sparkle by its reflection, skin so fair and unspotted. It is like seeing him again. It is good we are united. We are the remnants of a great family and we should share in its end."

"Had our family fewer pious men, perhaps the seed would have been more profusely sown," Héloïse remarked.

"The grace found in a celibate life is more than enough reward for pleasures lost," he assured her. "This you will learn when you join the nunnery and become my sister in Christ." Turning to the other maiden in the room, he noted, "I can see now by your dark locks and ruddy complexion my error in judging you my relative. What is your name?"

"Thessaly, sir," she sheepishly replied.

"Well, you both must be famished. Thessaly, go help my servant prepare some sustenance for us all," he commanded.

Thessaly picked up the bowls and commented, "Sir, he has already fixed some omelettes."

Fulbert dipped a finger in one of the bowls and put it to his lips, "Tastes more like hens turds than hens eggs!" he criticized. "Go, make a feast! I will celebrate the reunion of my family." Then directly to the monk he added, "Bring some fruit. I am fatigued." Thessaly and the servant went into the next room. Fulbert tasted the omelette once more and continued his complaint, "I do not know why his food tastes so. I have watched him wash the bowls and even the pot. For a long

43

time I thought that was the reason for the peculiar tang of his cuisine. I believe he does not wash the cloth that washes the pot. There is no flavour quite like it." He set the food aside, sat Héloïse down on a cushioned stool, and changed the subject by asking, "Now dear niece, how was your orphanage at the convent?"

"The sisters were good to me, if that's what you mean," she answered as a matter of fact.

"I regret that I did not see to your upbringing more personally," he explained. "But, as you can see, I do not live in an environment designed for a woman. My world is a world of men spending day and night studying the great works of ancient times and debating all sorts of theological concepts – hardly a place for a young maiden in a blue dress." He showed her a weighty manuscript and proceeded with his remarks, "This is my world, the divine struggle toward the acquirement of knowledge, the capture of dialectics, a boring life for a person like you. Surely, your female guardians taught you more practical and appropriate skills such as cooking and sewing."

"Well, no, Uncle," Héloïse stated. "The sisters taught me art and philosophy. We spent hours discussing current theology."

Fulbert responded condescendingly, "Ah, yes, a smattering of those disciplines is understandably necessary for a woman about to dedicate herself to the cloth. But fathomless thought is reserved for the deeper minds of men. God ordained it so."

"God . . . or man?" She retorted. "Is not the Church behind this deception? Many other cultures revered women. Did not Sabá have a queen that challenged the wisdom of Solomon? Did not Egypt's queen humble mighty Caesar? Are not the places in which we roam the infants of Mother Earth? Yet in Rome there is but papal father! Jesus took as a confidant the woman Mary Magdalene. Their intimate conversations went often beyond the understanding of the disciples, and she knew His needs better than any other who followed Him. Yet, the apostolic tradition suggests she was no more than a prostitute, unfairly belittling her since nowhere in the Gospel was she so labelled. As some think, if Jesus was associated with the Essenes, who were easily recognizable by the wearing of white garments, he probably held strong beliefs about the value of marriage and family. The affection that Jesus and Mary had for each other is obvious in the Bible. Jesus may have even taken her for His wife."

Fulbert winced at this notion. "Papal armies have slaughtered thousands in battle and burned hundreds at the stake for heresy less than this you have just proffered," he cautioned. "Do not express those thoughts aloud again, lest more sensitive ears pick them up. Our first Christian theologian, the apostle Paul, espoused the celibate life."

"Paul tried to sublimate man's weakness of flesh by degrading women," she retaliated. "Oh, to be Mary at the Master's side and hear the words straight from His mouth instead of the hearsay from a thousand years of masculine misinterpretation. I think shame would fall on all mankind if the truth was to be revealed."

"Perhaps I miscalculated your mental abilities," he said with a smile of approval. "I had hoped so."

"You impostor!" Héloïse scolded him after realizing she had just been tested. "Then it will be agreeable to you for me to study at the university?"

"I am not sure the university is ready for you," said Fulbert expressing concern. "Your feminine presence may prove disruptive during lectures. You may become a *disturbing* issue." Trying instantly to resolve this unexpected dilemma, Fulbert asserted, "We should have a scholastic privately tutor you and sharpen your mind before you are thrown to the dogmatic wolves. I know a young man who would be quite suitable, Alberic. I will ask him at the seminar tomorrow."

"May I attend at least this one seminar to meet my future instructor and assess those whose acceptance I must somehow gain?" she petitioned. "I promise to be inconspicuous."

"I doubt that's possible," said Fulbert raising his eyebrow again in amusement. Trying to envision the next day's events, he reasoned aloud, "Tomorrow may be unusual. Perhaps another time would be better."

"You will always say 'tomorrow' when the morrow comes if you wait for the soothsayer's consent," challenged Héloïse.

Seeing the strength of her argument, "Tomorrow, then," he reluctantly agreed.

The rest of the evening was spent enjoying the fine banquet that Thessaly and the servant had prepared, sharing light conversation, and rearranging Fulbert's house to accommodate the new residents. The two, Héloïse and Fulbert, finally had a home.

Chapter Five

Introductions

*M*y hand I should recoil, lest, like by a serpent, it is smitten.

This was a monumental day. It was the day I first met two important people in my life, Héloïse and Bernard. Along with a gathering of monks and students, I was waiting in the main assembly hall of the University for Fulbert's appearance. I was not expecting the guests he was about to present.

Abelard was also there, talking with a group of his cronies who were somewhat segregated from the rest. I had been visiting with them for a short while when Lotulpt, a new student who had quickly befriended me, came to draw my attention away from our idle conversation.

"I guess there will be some excitement around here today," he told me with a smile and in a hushed voice.

I began to question him further, "What do you mean?" but with a nudge to my shoulder he stopped further discussion and nodded toward the entrance of the hall.

Fulbert had arrived. He was trailed by a beautiful maiden whose advent caused a buzz from the swarm of men now assembled. From that point onward, I could not take my eyes off her. I was embarrassed by my fascination of her, and I prayed that my gawking was not obvious to her lest it would prove all the more awkward.

Fulbert greeted those in attendance with a thunderous voice designed to quiet the noisy crowd, "Good morning gentlemen."

"Good morning," responded many to his salutation.

"I hope it will not be an imposition upon you, my fellow scholastics, to ask that you indulge me the privilege of having my only kinfolk, my niece, Héloïse, here with me today," said Fulbert almost apologetically. "I promised her she might attend one of our seminars," he explained. "I trust you will find, as I have, that Héloïse has a most remarkable mind, for a woman, and that she can contribute to any of our discussions."

In an attempt to ingratiate myself to this new and charming visitor, and since I always had a comfortable and familiar relationship with my schoolmaster, I was the first to step forward to offer a light-hearted observation. "She is so much more attractive that you, dear Fulbert," I began, hoping to pique interest from Héloïse by my flattery, "I scarce believe she could be related. However, since you say so, if she has inherited a tenth of your intellect, I am sure it will be a pleasure to dwell in her company."

Héloïse subtly acknowledged my praise with a slight smile, but then I feared that she might just think me a glib fellow. Fulbert was not amused at all. "Thank you for that dubious compliment, Alberic," he said in a disapproving way.

Lotulpt rushed up to Fulbert with news. "Fulbert, Bernard is approaching," he announced.

Into the assembly hall marched Bernard of Clairvaux with an entourage of servant monks and scribes. He was a rather large figure, a little overweight for his small build. His thin, sandy-coloured hair almost gave him the appearance that he was bald, and his complexion was sweaty and ruddy from his brief exposure to the sun. Vigorously, he shook Fulbert's hands, "Greetings to you all," he exclaimed in a strident and far too loud voice for the occasion, "and especially to you, Fulbert, my old friend."

"It is good to see you again, honoured guest," the canon quietly replied.

"It is always good to return to this great university," he said for everyone to hear. He eyed Héloïse and whispered in the canon's ear, "Who is this maiden?"

As a formal introduction, Fulbert announced with a tad of pride in his voice, "Bernard, I would like you to meet my niece, Héloïse, a bright young woman who is eager to learn."

This time Bernard physically pulled Fulbert aside to sternly ask, "Are you sure these manly discussions are suitable for feminine ears?"

"Have no doubt that even though her body is more curvaceous than ours, her mind is as straight as any of us," Fulbert replied somewhat defensively.

"Well, we shall see," Bernard replied with reticence. "I have made a long journey," he added as he moved further into the crowd. As he passed by Lotulpt, Bernard handed him the cloak that he had just removed from around his shoulders, and stated, "Let us get on with the purpose for which I came."

"Yes, of course," said Fulbert obediently. He then moved up to the podium to give some introductory remarks. "Gentlemen, quiet, please," he began. "Today we are favoured to have with us a man many of you know personally or by repute, Bernard of Clairvaux. He is a respected scholastic and cleric who some feel should be the next French cardinal to Rome." Bernard, trying to display modesty, waved this comment off to the crowd. Fulbert continued by saying, "He is a righteous defender of the traditional values of the faith and believes in inner ecstasy through deep meditative communication with God." Fulbert concluded dryly, "He will address these topics… and other sundry matters."

Bernard bounded from his spot next to Lotulpt to accept the platform. "Thank you, most revered, Canon Fulbert," he began. "It is I who am favoured by being back in Paris to address such a distinguished assembly. As you know, I have had to be away from my beloved homeland because I was needed in Rome to assist with important Church affairs. For the present, however, I have returned to address important matters here." He paused and changed his countenance. "Fulbert mentioned that I am a righteous, and I am a relentless, defender of the traditional doctrines of the Christian religion. It is precisely the preservation of those precious tenets that has caused my premature exit from the courts of the Holy Empire. Word has come to me that our common beliefs are being perilously questioned by some of the younger, less experienced scholastics. I have come to express my views so that the light of my thoughts might dispel the darkness that has pervaded the minds of those who may have unwittingly heard and followed those who speak untruths." He stepped away from the dais to make his next point. "It is the passion of change and youth which has brought about the degradation of Christian values today," he loudly pronounced. "It is not the will of God."

Lotulpt shouted out, "Tell us, then, what *is* the will of God?"

Bernard circumvented the query by saying, "The will of God will remain elusive to those who do not believe in Him. It will be hidden from those who do not abide His truths."

Almost as if on cue, Lotulpt again chimed in, "What are these truths and how do we know them?"

Once more, Bernard did not give a direct answer. "Truth is not easily found," he said. "There are too many forces that work to cloud it, too many temptations to distract us from it. One must suffer torment and moments of self-deprivation to find it. All men cannot muster the strength and self-control to uncover it. Only, those, pure of heart, who are devoted to meditation and deep intuitive penetration, can possibly achieve the knowledge of truth."

Abelard emerged from the crowd for the first time to ask, "Then is there no hope for the sinner? Will he forever be unable to find truth?"

"Because of his sin, truth is lost to him," Bernard asserted definitively.

"But if the sinner, who, by virtue of birth, you would say all men are, cannot know the truth, then how can he know of his sins?" Abelard questioned further.

Bernard remained calm and resolutely answered Abelard's inquiry by noting, "Not all men have the faculties to discover truth. That is why some of us are called to convey the truth to those less capable. It is our responsibility to point out their sin and help purge it from their souls."

Abelard was becoming quite troubled by Bernard's statements and said in frustration, "I know of only one man authorized to purge sin from the souls of men. They called him Christ!"

"Be quiet, Abelard. Do not offend a great man!" warned Lotulpt.

"It is not I who made the offence, nor is he the great One to take offence. It is the greatest of us all who has been offended," said Abelard to rebuke Lotulpt for his sycophantic attitude toward Bernard.

"I do not presume to play Christ," Bernard warranted. "I am, such as the apostles, merely His representative."

Almost in a snide tone, Abelard countered, "Then are these so-called 'representatives' the sole determiners of God's truth?"

Lotulpt and a couple of others from the crowd moved menacingly toward Abelard and were about to lay hands on him to evict him from the premises. Bernard shook his head to stop their actions, for he was satisfied with his response, "No one determines God's truth except God."

Coming boldly forward to face Bernard, Abelard put another question to him. "Then, sir, if God's truth is His own, why could he not reveal it in any manner of His choosing?" he asked, "Why not through man's own power to reason?"

Bernard sneered outwardly at the suggestion. "That is quite simple," he began. Then, glaring at Abelard, he delivered his response readily, "Reason is the ploy of the Devil. It is his means to outwit and disconcert you. Reason is based on earthly experiences and knowledge, and the earth is the domain of the Devil. Only the soul is the domain of God. Truth is perceived only through the soul."

Abelard started to protest, "I am sorry, but I must differ..."

Bernard confronted him immediately by shouting, "Would you allow truth to be dictated by each man according to his own reasoning? Why, there would be chaos, and God's truth would be forever lost because man's truth would be selfishly conceived."

Genuinely trying to explain, Abelard proceeded, "Not at all. Each man's reason has similarities with each other man's reason. Just as men have a common soul, so, too, do all men have common reason. Precisely, by discovering the common elements of man's reasoning can we discover God's universal truths."

"Universal truths through reason are truths of Satan," stated Bernard emphatically.

"You cannot shatter the logic of Bernard, Abelard," interjected Lotulpt. "Truth based on reason is the same as truth based on the Devil, and we all know how well the Devil is recognized for telling the truth!" There were timid chuckles rambling through the crowd at Lotulpt's remark.

"It is not the Devil who created us, Lotulpt, at least not most of us." That retort from Abelard, this time, brought outward laughter amid those in attendance. "It was God the creator who implanted common parts into a man, a common body, with a common soul, and a common ability to reason."

"I will not tolerate further blasphemy!" bellowed Bernard, his voice echoing against the arches above. He motioned his servants to exit and prepared for an ostentatious departure without another word.

Abelard would not give in to such a pedantic display and said, almost tauntingly, "Blasphemy cannot be judged by man because men do not know what is offensive to God's ear!"

Bernard gave a flippant response over his shoulder to Abelard as he was stomping toward the doorway, "I will pray for you, my son!"

Calling back to him, "Pray not for me, but for understanding," Abelard uttered unrepentantly.

With that, Bernard stopped, pivoted around, and glared threateningly at Abelard. "I *un-der-stand* that you are a spokesman for the Devil!" he scolded. "You tread upon dangerous ground, and I would be afraid of losing my immortal soul if I were you." Then he addressed the rest of the crowd, "Remove this plague carrier from your midst before you are all contaminated!"

Fulbert rushed to Bernard and tried to temper his wrath by saying, "Dear Bernard, this man is a friend to everyone here, including me. He is not an evil man, as you suggest. His youth is probably responsible for his impetuous behaviour. Perhaps all of us should be more open to new thoughts that might bring us closer to God."

"Fulbert, have you also been taken in by this defiler of God?" accused Bernard.

Fulbert meekly protested the notion, "No, I did not mean..."

"I came here to speak the truth, not debate it!" growled Bernard. "I have no use for this company. I will be on my way." He counselled Fulbert, "Rid yourself of this menace. I have a grave foreboding that he has a dark destiny."

"I hope his fate is not darkened by the shadow of your hand," expressed the distressed canon gravely.

"It will be by the hand of God," proclaimed Bernard. "Good day, Fulbert." Then, he called back to the others loud enough to be heard over the commotion that had filled the room, "Farewell to you all. I pray those who are obedient followers of the faith will make their way out of this pit of sin. Farewell again I say. For I tell you, you shall not see me again until the serpent is removed from its den." With that statement, he finally departed.

Lotulpt broke the silence that had overtaken the crowd after Bernard's parting remark. "Wait, Bernard, we will go too," he called.

Others began to leave quickly, saying, "Yes, let's go with Bernard."

Bernard was already out of sight when Fulbert said softly, "Fare thee well, friend. May God go with you and with your understanding." Then, turning to Abelard, he chided, "Woe to us all, and especially you, Abelard, for offending such a powerful man!"

Abelard wanted to defend his actions to the schoolmaster for whom he had so much respect and explained, "I only spoke the truth as I know it through my own reasoning..."

Fulbert had enough of this discourse and concluded, "I know all about your truth through reason, but I am too tired to argue for or against it. Yet, I find no fault in your words or their sincerity. Any means that brings man closer to God cannot be a work of the Devil. I know yours is a pious search for God's truth. But, be warned! New ideas take time to grow in the minds of others. Men have their own ideas and these ideas are as precious to them as yours is to you. You face a formidable opponent in Bernard. His theology is not only his own, but that of the Church and this university."

"Canon Fulbert, I understand your admonition and appreciate it," said Abelard in a warm manner to his teacher. "I will try to be less flagrant in presenting my views. However, I cannot abandon them."

"Your views are your own," responded the empathetic Fulbert. "No one can take them from you." He waved a warning finger as he said, "But watch your tongue lest someone takes that from you."

"I shall seal my lips and lock my tongue inside," quipped Abelard.

"Good, see that you do," replied the canon as he looked around for his niece who had been listening from the safety of an alcove far away from Bernard's tirade. "Come, Héloïse, we might as well go. Any chance for this to be a normal session has long vanished." He began to leave.

Hurriedly catching up to him, she asked, "Uncle, may I stay a while to walk the halls and gardens?"

Fulbert eyed her suspiciously before answering, "Yes, my dear, but beware of things beyond your understanding."

She knew that Fulbert suspected her true motive for wanting to stay so, feeling caught in a lie, she answered with a blush to her face, "Yes, uncle."

"Alberic, take charge of my niece and see that she is delivered back to me within the hour," Fulbert ordered.

I was glad to oblige. "Yes, within the hour," I iterated to show that I grasped completely his instructions.

Upon Fulbert's departure, most of those remaining departed, too, except for a group still talking with Abelard. Héloïse grabbed my arm and coaxed me to follow, saying, "Let's go listen to what they are discussing."

I reluctantly followed her lead to the huddled group of about fifteen monks and students that had encircled Abelard. They did not seem disturbed, or even paid much notice, when we joined them.

Abelard was in mid thought saying, "And, so, my friends, we must reject those tyrannical theologians who insist that God is their exclusive property and they, as landlords, can dictate what price we must pay for our spiritual existence."

A young and loyal follower of Abelard spoke up, "We are with you, Abelard, and believe what you are saying. But give our minds a rest! Sing one of your songs for us."

"John of Salisbury, John, my beloved, you were so aptly christened," noted Abelard. "For as John of so long ago did for the Master, how often you take my troubled heart and make it want to sing again by your faithfulness and child-like innocence. For you I will sing." Abelard prefaced his song with an explanation about its timeliness. "Many of you will hear this as an Advent song celebrating our Lord's birth, and it is," he asserted. "Why I would sing it now, when spring fills the world with life instead of during the traditional season when winter covers the world with cold death, I shall elucidate." John brought him a bow and box lyre that Abelard rested on his lap and, then, upon which he rested his arms.

"The variations between the many calendars in use from ancient times to the present have caused serious inaccuracies in determining the duration of the year," he began as if lecturing. "As some of you might have studied in astronomy, the fact is that a solar year cannot be evenly divided by days, weeks, or months. So, early calendars based on the phases of the moon, or months, eventually did not agree with the seasons. Then, sometimes a month had to be added to reconcile the differences. The ancient Roman calendar became hopelessly confused when officials, to whom were entrusted the task of adding days and months to correct such inconsistencies, abused their authority to prolong their own terms of office or delay elections by arbitrarily adding time to the official calendar. Many scholars now believe that the inaccuracies were so great that our Lord, Jesus Christ, did not usher in the Christian era by his nativity in the first year Anno Domini, but in the fourth anno prior to his reported birth, and probably not in December, but most likely in April. So, on this lovely April day, it is appropriate to celebrate His birth."

"Must you even challenge the Pope's calendar?" teased one of the students.

"I do what I must," Abelard replied guardedly.

Abelard began to sing in a smooth tenor voice that broke easily into falsetto on the high notes,

> *"Journeyed from Nazareth to Bethlehem's plain,*
> *Jesu is born, Jesu is born,*
> *Prophesy filled, the correct lineage to reign,*
> *Born the Son of David.*
>
> *Laid to rest in a manger bed,*
> *Jesu is born, Jesu is born,*
> *Born of the virgin who cradled his head,*
> *Born the son of Mary."*

The group began to hum the tune with Abelard.

> *His birth was heralded by Gabriel on high,*
> *Jesu is born, Jesu is born,*
> *Songs from the angelic host filled the sky,*
> *Born the King of Heaven.*
> *Wise men and shepherds at the stable now meet,"*

With a nod, Abelard invited the others to sing the repeated line,

> *"Jesu is born, Jesu is born,*
> *Bringing him gifts, they bow at his feet,*
> *Born the king of men.*
>
> *This infant brings a message of love,*
> *Jesu is born, Jesu is born,*
> *A wondrous gift from the Father above,*
> *Born the Son of God."*

As the song neared its end, Abelard slowed the tempo and sang in a reflective mood. He seemed to address the verse toward Héloïse.

> *"An innocent born with a cross to bear,*
> *Jesu is born, Jesu is born,*
> *Our sins forgive, our souls to spare,*
> *Born the saviour of men."*

There was applause from the group and John suggested, "Sing another, Abelard."

"No, no," politely refused Abelard, "Your time here is to be spent on much more serious matters. Go back to your studies and prayers. We will have other days. Good day to you all." He stood as if to leave while the others departed, but then came over to Héloïse and me. "Fulbert did me an injustice by not introducing me to his niece. Thus far, we have been only told that your name is Héloïse, is that correct?" he said with a slight bow.

"Yes," she answered, holding forth her hand to him, "And, from what I gathered from Bernard's remarks, you must be the devil, Abelard, from whom my hand I should recoil, lest, like by a serpent, it is smitten."

"Fear not, for there is no venom in this serpent by which to do you harm," Abelard assured her. "Come and sit down." Héloïse followed him to a wooden bench where the two of them sat close to one another. "I must apologize for my actions today," Abelard said. "Forgive my outrageous display."

"I am not sure you need any forgiveness," replied Héloïse. "I listened carefully to what you said and found nothing repulsive in it. Do you really believe that man's reason can be an instrument to find God?"

"Yes, I do," affirmed Abelard.

"Then what about woman?" she questioned. "What about the woman who is not given the opportunity to learn, to understand, and to reason? Is woman forever relegated to menial service to man? Are we to live in darkness without the light of truth unless man conveys it to us? Is this less tyrannical than one man saying he knows God's truth better than another?"

Abelard gently interrupted, "It is a widely held belief that women are incapable of reason..."

Jumping to her feet furiously, "Why, that is ridiculous!" she countered irritably. "Just as you find the theology of Bernard intolerable, so must I find your concept of man's reason being superior to woman's."

Abelard tried to sooth her by saying, "Wait, wait, let me finish." He pulled her down beside him again. "I merely said it was common thinking that a woman's mind is not keen on reasoning..." Héloïse started to react, but he quickly continued, "Yet, I believe that in a woman's mind has been locked away an even better understanding of God than in man's. Woman has been less warlike, less proud, and less arrogant. She has been more subservient, more healing, more loving. Who, then, is more like the loving Christ who washed the Disciples feet? Cruel man or gentle woman? Who, then, can better comprehend the nature of God, the master or the servant, the destroyer of life or the bearer of it? Do not desire to trade your lot with men's, for you fare far better than he when it comes to obtaining the keys to Heaven's gate."

Héloïse had listened attentively to all that Abelard had told her and replied, "Forgive me for being so easy to accuse. I am ashamed."

"There is nothing of which to be ashamed," said Abelard. "You have had your whole life to think nothing but the worst of us men."

"You are different. It was foolish of me to think that all men are the same," she apologized.

John scampered back into the chamber and, almost out of breath from excitement, he interrupted the two, "You must go and defend yourself. Bernard is up to some tricks. He has reassembled a large contingent of supporters on the other side of the campus and is spewing theology to them that is designed to discredit you and turn those gathered against you."

"Patience, John," said Abelard calmly. "Tomorrow Bernard will be bound for the next school and crowd to impress. There will be another day and another time for me to argue against him, but I shall go and listen from afar about the atrocities he claims I have committed. I am sorry, I must go," he told Héloïse.

Trying to think of something to keep him from leaving, she offered, "My uncle said I may be tutored by a local scholar if I wish, and if I can find one who would teach a woman. It is such a lowly task."

Abelard paused from his exit to agree, "It would be a deplorable task."

They both laughed, then, Héloïse proposed, "You will teach me, won't you?"

"I will if you think me qualified, and if Fulbert gives his wholehearted consent," said Abelard setting forth his conditions.

"I think you'll do," she jested, "And, Fulbert will be satisfied with my choice."

John beckoned to Abelard and pleaded, "We should go!"

"When do we begin?" asked Abelard as he was being shoved toward the door by John.

"Tomorrow," responded Héloïse. Then wondering if she was rushing things, she asked, "Is that too soon?"

"No, tomorrow will be fine," called Abelard, as his friend was forcing him onward. "Wait. Fulbert will be lecturing tomorrow. Will you be there?"

"I will be there," she called back even though he had already disappeared through the door. She looked at me and with a smile asked, "Alberic, would you walk with me through the gardens before I must go home?"

Chapter Six

The Parable

*W*hy could not this young man immediately recognize and act spontaneously toward that which he so earnestly sought?

It was one of those beautiful and balmy spring days. I know that spring always seems exceptional after the long and dismal winter, however, this particular day was so magnificent that one could not help but take notice of it.

Fulbert decided to meet on a grassy knoll outside the city along the west bank of the Seine, which was something he frequently had our class do. This was a practice based upon the teaching style of Christ who often taught his disciples in pleasant outdoor settings. Alone, I had come early knowing that Fulbert was prone to arrive at these lessons before his students. My hunch paid off when I saw at a distance the fair Héloïse accompanying him to this spot earlier than the predetermined time. I knew she would somehow manage to get consent from her uncle to attend this lecture. Never had the spring air been so full of flowery fragrance, nor the breeze moved so caressingly as it brushed through her billowing golden hair.

"Magnificent, is it not?" came a voice from behind me.

Reeling around in astonishment, I answered, "Abelard, you. Uh, yes, magnificent."

"This wonderful weather or the view?" he questioned in jest as he went off to greet others who were also arriving.

To my dismay, it seemed that every student that day had come early for Fulbert's lesson. The knoll was littered with the entire assembly even before the master had made his way to the focal point of the area, which was a large, solitary stone at the highest point of the knoll.

Fulbert sat upon the rock while Héloïse deposited herself on the ground next to him and leaned her straight, strong back against the side of the stone.

Then, to introduce the lesson topic for the day, Fulbert began by saying, "You will recall that last week we spoke about the effectiveness of Jesus' teaching by his use of the parable. Now, the parable was not a new form of teaching when our Lord so masterfully utilized it to illuminate spiritual truths. Greek rhetoricians gave the name 'parable' to their literary illustrations centuries before Christ's birth. Christ took the parable to its highest level as an aid in comprehending the most difficult of concepts, making them both simple for those who are weak in understanding and yet complex enough to challenge the most disciplined mind. I asked you each to try to come up with your own parable to express some truth about which you feel deeply. Alberic, do you have one to share?"

Fulbert often asked me first when it came to eliciting responses from the class. He must have done this because he was confident in my complete preparedness for the class, a trait that set a good example for others less diligent in their studies. If he did not start a class discussion with my input, it would be with Abelard's.

I rose from the soft, grassy spot where I had been comfortably sitting to address the class and my mentor. I was not as apt at storytelling like some of those in my class, but this parable had come to me one night as sort of a dreamy revelation and I felt its theme's validity was without question. This belief bolstered my courage enough to deliver it with a sense of authority.

"A young man heard of this good and wise teacher and set out to seek him. People had given the young man only vague directions as to where this teacher may be found. Early one day in his travels however, he came upon a man sowing his garden and asked, 'Do you know where I might find this great teacher I have heard so much about?'

'Yes,' replied the gardener.

'Will you tell me, please, how to find him then?' implored the young man.

'You still have a long way to go,' cautioned the gardener, 'But I will tell you. Follow the road on which you tread. After a few miles you will come to a fork in the road. Take the path on the right and, after a while, it will lead you to the river. There is a much narrower path that follows the river. Take the path that goes upstream with the river. It becomes yet narrower but leads to a higher ground. When you reach the high ground, you will see your destination.'

The young man thanked the gardener and went on his way. He followed the directions carefully. He took the right path. He travelled the upstream trail even though it became narrow and difficult in step along the rocky ledges. He reached the high ground and looked out over a beautiful plain. The journey had taken most of the day. It was growing dark. He was tired. He followed an ever-widening road that led into the plain. Before long, he came upon a man tending his flock of sheep. 'Hey, you!' called the young man. 'I am lost and need some help.'

The shepherd approached the young man who was amazed to find that he was the gardener with whom he had spoken to earlier. 'I must have made a wrong turn somewhere,' stammered the young man, 'For I find myself in the same place from where I first began.'

'No,' replied the shepherd. 'You must have followed correctly, for you have found whom you seek.'

'If that is so,' questioned the young man, 'Why did you have me travel my whole day, over narrow paths and rocky ledges, to end up where I already was?'

'Indeed, my son,' replied the shepherd, 'Had the way been easy, would the arrival have been as great?'"

I sat back down upon the spot where the grass had already been flattened earlier by the weight of my presence. The group was disconcertingly quiet. I glanced at Abelard who gave me a smile and a nod of understanding. I hoped the silence was due to the others being so absorbed in the story just related that they were still in deep contemplation about its meaning.

"Very interesting," remarked Fulbert. "Are there any comments?"

Lotulpt spoke up first, "I think it is a fine parable. It vividly portrays man's life-long search for God."

Demurely, Héloïse asked, "Is it all right if I make a comment?"

Fulbert hesitated but motioned his consent with a shrug of his shoulders and a dip of his head.

"I wonder," began Héloïse, "If the young man in the parable can be compared to the rich young ruler who asked the Lord how he might gain eternal life? Jesus named the commandments one by one and the young man had broken none. He had followed all the directions and yet he left in sorrow because he was truly unable to find a relationship with God or man."

Abelard quickly added a comment, which he directed to me, "What is then the worth of the fishermen and tax collector who dropped everything when asked to 'Follow me'? Why could not this young man immediately recognize and act spontaneously toward that which he so earnestly sought?"

"Because a parable is limited in scope and usually serves to illustrate only a single point," concluded Fulbert. "Alberic's point is not without validity. All right then, do you have a parable we can critique, Abelard?"

Abelard rose to his feet and began his tale.

"There was a good king who had created his beloved kingdom by his own hands. And, although this kingdom was great, one day he heard cries of despair from his people. He summoned the servants of his court and asked of them, 'Why do the people cry out?'

'They cry out because of want and need for the rich blessings only their king can bestow upon them,' observed one of the servants.

'Then empty the treasury and storehouses. I will pour out all that I have onto them so that their want may be satisfied.' And with that statement, the king sent out his servants to do his bidding.

When the servants returned, the king assembled them and asked if they had done all he had commanded them, and every servant answered that they had. 'Then why do I still hear my people crying out so desperately?' he asked.

'It is such, sire,' answered one of the chief servants, 'That their wants cannot be satisfied.'

'You mean that all the riches of my kingdom could not surely satisfy them,' asked the puzzled king.

'We did not give them all of your riches!' explained another one of the chief servants, 'For we knew they would only squander them and make us all the poorer by their foolish liberality and lack of understanding of what you had done for them.'

'You wicked and disobedient servants!' shouted the angry king. 'You, who know best the riches of my kingdom because I have freely shared them with you and have asked only that you share them likewise with others, you I cast into the dungeon's darkest depths. You shall cry out to me, but I will not hear you. For I, myself, shall go out to the people and be among them.'"

With their eyes focused on Fulbert, the group of students remained silent as Abelard sat upon the ground once more.

Fulbert grimaced and changed position upon the rock to relieve some discomfort brought about by his prolonged sitting in one place during Abelard's story. "I think we will dispense with any discussion about this parable," he suggested. "Besides, the afternoon has worn on and I have other plans for all of you." From a leather sack he always carried, Fulbert pulled out a round fruit that he began to peel. He bit into a segment of its soft interior and juice and aroma filled the air. Holding up the remainder of the fruit, he proclaimed, "Another debt of gratitude I owe the Moors." The fruit was an exotic and costly delicacy, and I was always struck by this luxury he afforded himself. He seemed to never be without it, even in the dead of winter when it must have been even harder to procure.

Refreshed from his snack, Fulbert gave directions, "Alberic and Abelard, choose up sides from among your peers, for I have an experiment to perform."

I quickly enlisted Lotulpt and some of his friends to be on my team while others went to Abelard and joined him. With curiosity I watched Abelard as he and his followers approached Fulbert. "May Héloïse join our group, Master Fulbert?" Abelard asked.

Why hadn't I thought of doing that? I was disappointed that I had not been the first to include her, and I stepped forward to make my case by pleading, "Had I known Héloïse was to be part of your experiment, master, I would have immediately requested that she join our group. Nonetheless, it appears I am one or two short of having an equal number in my troupe as is in Abelard's, so she should rightfully be mine."

Fulbert glanced at Héloïse who, I think, glanced at Abelard, and then responded with, "The right is with he who asked first. It is not important whether or not the sides are of equal strength, for this is not a competition, only a learning experience. True strength does not lie in numbers anyway, but in wisdom. And that is what we are striving to acquire. Alberic and Abelard, come to me."

Fulbert pulled Abelard down to him and whispered something in his ear, and then whispered into mine. "I have assigned each of these two a task," he announced to the rest of the class. "Go with the one whom you have chosen to lead you. He will explain further what you are supposed to do. Two days hence, return here and report what you have discovered."

With that assignment to his class, Fulbert rose to begin his descent to the path that led to the city. He paused to address

Abelard. "Again some advice; if what you say publicly is going to cause only controversy, like that parable of yours, try to avoid saying it, for your words will not always fall upon sympathetic ears."

"Then I would have nothing to say at all," objected Abelard, "For it seems no matter what I say is controversial in the minds of some."

Fulbert shook his head and continued down the knoll with Héloïse following.

"Wait," called Abelard, "Do I not get Héloïse to stay and be part of my group?"

"You may retrieve her tomorrow," answered Fulbert as he held forth his arm to escort Héloïse on their way. The two groups also set out on their separate ways, I leading one, and Abelard leading the other, to do our master's bidding.

Chapter Seven

The Pledge

*L*et us not be victims of circumstance, but victors over our own destinies.

The morrow was not quite as perfect a day as the previous one. My group set off on the quest Fulbert had sent us. So, did Abelard's, and Héloïse brought back to me all the details of her adventure.

Before getting started on their mission, Abelard, John, and four others from the class got some provisions together and made their last stop Fulbert's house to pick up Héloïse. It was just at first light when the small troupe was making their way through the empty streets of the city. The morning was so tranquil that it instilled an attitude of quietness among them. As if to break the spell of silence the morning had cast upon them, John whispered to Abelard "Getting up this early is for the birds." Abelard made no comment, but the others continued their stealthy walk and hushed conversation all the way to Fulbert's house. Upon reaching the door, Abelard knocked so loudly that his companions were startled by its resonance.

Héloïse had been watching for their approach and was at the door before Abelard had a chance to knock a second time. "I am ready," she answered to his loud rapping as she opened the door to exit, "There is no need to disturb the master with your impertinent noise!"

"It was merely a knock on the door," he explained.

"But did it need be so bold?" she gently chided him, and she skipped off in front of the group as if to take lead of the expedition. "Come along, now," she beckoned, "The day will be spent before we know it."

John shrugged his shoulders and smiled at Abelard. Abelard nodded with a scowl in Héloïse's direction and the company scampered off to join her.

"Well, brave sojourner, when are you going to tell us about our mission?" Héloïse asked Abelard as she pranced beside him in exuberance.

"In about forty," he answered with a big smile to John.

John and the rest of the group had heard that reply from Abelard many times before and knew exactly what he meant. However, for Héloïse, his response was slightly irritating. Stopping mid stride she asked, "What kind of answer is that?"

"It is the best you are going to get from him for now," chuckled John as he continued walking at Abelard's side.

Héloïse trotted to catch up with the two compeers, "Well sir that is not a good enough answer."

Abelard was not annoyed and explained, "We are to go nowhere but everywhere, to learn nothing or everything."

"Now, is that more clear, Héloïse?" laughed John. "You may as well be patient and wait until he is ready to tell you what he wants you to know."

Héloïse pouted only briefly and then silently resigned herself to Abelard's secretive ways.

The sun was beginning to pound the earth with its penetrative rays. It was steaming away the dew left from the moist night and was awakening the flora still droopy from its long slumber. The city was also showing more signs of life. People were stirring from their sleep. The air was filled with the aroma of home fires and the smoke carried with it the scent of break-fast delicacies. One could hear now the clogging of horse's hooves on distant cobblestone streets. The birds seemed particularly noisy in their banter to one another from across tree to tree. Abelard tarried in the midst of all this morning activity and looked to the right, then the left, then behind him, and finally to Héloïse. "How lovely is the morning," he reflected, "God's re-creation of the first day."

"Yes, its freshness and newness seem to renew the spirit as well," observed Héloïse.

The gardens of the city exhibited the best of nature's art this spring. Every domicile along the street was decorated with blooming flowers and trees. "Look at the pear and plum trees veiled of white," commented Abelard.

"And the cherry dressed in its bridal gown," added Héloïse.

"To attract its suitor bee!" quipped John. The others in the group snickered at his somewhat bawdy allusion.

Abelard was oblivious to the group's reaction to John's remark and had moved toward a carefully tended garden on the corner lot of a wealthy merchant's home. He trespassed upon the grounds and Héloïse quickly followed. The two of them walked the garden paths together, stopping often to smell one of the many fragrant blooms. A servant from the house approached them. Soon the master of the house popped out and quickly headed straight for the two interlopers. Héloïse was a little concerned that Abelard and she might be the centre of an unpleasant incident by their trespassing.

"Maybe we should be on our way," she suggested.

Abelard was bending over to pick a small, but exquisite, rose. "I'll handle this," he assured her as he handed Héloïse the fresh-cut flower.

Giving the rose back to Abelard, Héloïse exclaimed, "I do not want to hold the evidence of your crime!"

"Abelard, dear friend," the merchant called out, "How good to see you." When he finally reached the two he asked, "How is my son doing?"

"Your son is doing well. He is a bright student. He will be a great scholastic someday and will make you proud."

"Coming from you, Abelard, I consider that a high compliment," said the beaming merchant.

"And I must compliment you," added Abelard, "For being a man of wisdom and allowing your son to pursue his innermost aspiration."

The merchant smiled and asked, "Was there something you needed?"

"No, no, only this rose," answered Abelard.

"The whole garden is yours, dear friend," the merchant declared, "My house, my food, all of it is yours for the taking. None of it is enough to repay the debt I owe you."

"Thank you, my friend, but this rose is enough. Now I must get back to my friends who are waiting for my return." With that, Abelard turned to join the others with Héloïse following closely behind.

When the group had reassembled, Héloïse asked Abelard, "What great debt does this rich man owe you?"

"Abelard cast out his son's demons," answered John for Abelard.

"It is nothing," Abelard cautioned Héloïse as he pinched off the thorns from the rose's stem.

"Nothing?" responded John in disagreement. "Why the son was possessed of devils and so violent that no one dared pass his way. When Abelard heard of this, he rushed to the merchant's house. Without a word, Abelard grabbed one of the merchant's young pigs from its pen and, with pig in arms, swiftly entered the house to the astonishment of everyone present. He dismissed the merchant and his servants from the house and entered into the son's bedchamber. After much loud shouting from the room, the squealing pig ran wildly from the house, passed the bewildered merchant and his servants, and disappeared out of sight."

"His malady was of the mind, not the body," remarked Abelard dryly.

"The boy came out from his room with a calm and serene demeanour unlike any the family had witnessed from him before," continued John. "And, moreover, the pig was found the next day floating dead in the Seine!"

Héloïse's eyes were open wide and her mouth was still agape from listening so intently to this quite incredible story.

Abelard turned to her and said, "The rose, a diminutive member of the family when compared to its lofty relatives the cherry, the pear, and the plum, nonetheless puts its kinfolk to shame by its incomparable beauty."

He placed the flower gently into Héloïse's hair. It was the first time he had touched her and his hand lingered longer than necessary upon her silky locks. Of course he had looked at Héloïse before that moment, but never as deeply into her eyes. A revelation came over him that he felt compelled to express, "Yet even the rose pales in comparison to thee."

Everyone, including Héloïse, was shocked by Abelard's flattery but chose to ignore it. Héloïse quickly broke away from the mutual fixation between her and Abelard and asked, "When are we going to begin the mission on which my uncle sent us?"

"In about forty," the others, except Abelard, responded in chorus.

"Follow me," Abelard directed. He led the group a short distance to the edge of the Seine. "Look upon the banks of the river that are blanketed in the purple of the heartsease. Even royalty is not cloaked as elegantly."

The expedition left the city and continued north along the river. As the group travelled at a steady and assured pace, Abelard would make other such comments as, "Examine the rolling pasture made golden by the buttercups. Even the streets of Heaven are envious of its brilliance."

Under Abelard's leadership the small band went northwest of the city into a large wooded area known as the Forêt de Rouvray. Abelard would stop to smell the various wildflowers he spotted along the way. Superb specimens he would pick and give to Héloïse until she bore a large and beautiful bouquet. The potent fragrance from it made them all feel dizzy with enchantment.

Around noontime the troupe ate as they continued on their journey – not pausing a moment. A member of the group later told me that Abelard seemed to be getting more and more enraptured with the flowers around him, especially one particular flower in full bloom – Héloïse. Abelard was twenty years older than she, almost forty, yet the blush of youth still lingered on his cheek. His appearance and vitality did not betray his age. He was tall and, although lean, very strong. He once took me on a visit to his homeland. After meeting his family, it was obvious he received his knightly stature from his father, but his intellect and amicability from his mother. His privileged home life was in direct contrast with the harsh peasant life I knew as a youth. I do not know if his intent was to honour me as a guest in his home or to dishonour me by the comparison of his house to mine. So it was with Abelard; it was always hard to read his intentions. John and the rest of the group probably took Abelard's attention to Héloïse as patriarchal and thought no more of it. She, on the other hand, may have thought differently.

The group traversed on until the shadows of the trees grew long upon the sojourners' path. Coming to an open area where the path had been widened by some woodman's axe, Abelard suggested, "Let's stay here for the night and tomorrow return to Paris."

"The day is not yet lost," remarked one of the students, "We can get back to the city before the watchman closes the gate. Besides, we have not made provision for staying the night in the woods."

Abelard turned to Héloïse and privately told her, "Be not concerned, for I explained to Fulbert aforehand what I intended to do." He, then, proclaimed to the others, "Be it not my decision, but let the fairest among us choose. If she can meet the challenge without trepidation, then how much more should you display manly bravery? Héloïse may decide."

"The night gets cold, Héloïse," warned one of the reluctant compeers.

"We have no food to eat," cautioned another.

"There are sharp-toothed animals in the woods to nibble on you at night," teased John with a big smile that revealed his own canines.

"As entertaining as it sounds, I think we should return . . ." Héloïse paused, smiled, and then finished her sentence, "Tomorrow!"

The men groaned and began to complain. "Let's make camp, then, you hardy men," coaxed Abelard. "Collect wood for a fire, and find logs upon which to sit. We are better equipped than you might suspect, for John has brought with him a full skin of wine, a slab of cheese, and loaves of bread to celebrate this special occasion."

Everyone went to work straightaway, and, as night closed in, the troupe huddled around a blazing fire to share in the warmth, the wine, and each other's banter. They laughed together and Abelard sang them songs. When the evening had worn on, and the light-hearted conversation had lagged, Héloïse could resist no longer, "When are you going to tell us about our reason for being here?" she asked.

"In about forty," repeated Abelard as he rose to his feet and set out into the darkness of the surrounding woods.

"Why does he keep saying that?" an annoyed Héloïse asked John.

He finally explained, "Poor Noah had it rain upon him for forty days and forty nights before he beheld the rainbow. Moses' people wandered in the wilderness for forty years before reaching the Promised Land. And Jesus endured the temptations of Satan for forty days in the desert before returning to Jordan in full Spirit. 'In about forty' is Abelard's way of saying 'be patient,' 'persevere,' and good things will come forth in the end."

Héloïse got up to go find Abelard. "He often goes off by himself like that," remarked John. "I have gone with him before in mid night, only to fall asleep while he keeps vigil. I do not know for what he is watching or waiting. You might as well wait for his return."

Héloïse entered the forest in the same general direction as Abelard and was quickly swallowed up by the darkness. She listened for sounds of movement through the thicket that might help her set a course to him, but heard none. Her eyes were almost useless in the hunt for Abelard, yet her ears were attuned to any noise that now seemed doubly loud against the absolute quiet of the wilderness. She was so sensitized that a twig broken under the lightest footstep would be perceived by her as a mighty timber snapped by Zephyr's fury. Surely no stealth could withstand detection from her keen sense. She went deeper into the woods until she began to feel uncomfortable about the distance she had travelled without considering a return route. She stopped, stayed motionless, and listened intently for the first audible clue to her whereabouts in relation to the camp or to Abelard.

"What are you doing here?" came a deep voice from behind her.

Héloïse took a giant leap forward and then turned to confront Abelard. Gasping for breath she answered, "I came to find out what you may be doing out here."

"You were not invited to follow me," scolded Abelard. "You should not have left the safety of the fire and your companions. You could easily lose yourself in the deep unknown."

"I am not afraid. Besides, I know a good shepherd who would leave his flock to find the one who is lost."

"You are rare amongst maidens," he noted. "Come with me." Abelard grabbed her long, smooth hand and escorted her through the overgrowth of wild grasses and prickly branches that kept trying to impede the couple's progress by seizing onto their arms and legs. After a short distance, the woodland gave way to a rocky ledge near the bank of the river. He brought her to the very edge of a massive, flat stone jutting out over the water in order to get a better vantage point of the sky and said, "Just look at the moon."

"The moon?" questioned Héloïse, "Why do you think it is so dark tonight? There is no moon upon which to gaze."

"Oh, but there is! It is a new moon, and even if you can't see it, it is still there and is nonetheless wonderful." He moved close behind her and lifted her arms skyward, instructing her to sight with them, and said, "It is above us at the tip of your fingers."

She peered into the black sky and said, "I think I see it too." She pivoted to face Abelard and asked, "But how do you know where to look?"

"Ah, that is the trick for many things," replied Abelard. Then, with a shudder, he realized, "The air is cold. You must be freezing. Let me take you back to the fire."

"Not yet. It is warm here." Héloïse pivoted again to press her back into Abelard. There was silence for a while. Abelard slowly inched his arms around Héloïse and the warmth became more intense. "Talk to me," she whispered.

"About what?" he asked softly.

"About the thoughts that immerse your mind when you wander out on your own such as this, in your solitude," she replied.

"I think of life, do you not?" he asked.

"Yes, and what of it?" she prodded.

Abelard thought for a moment and then decided to continue, "On a beautiful day like we have had today, I see evidence that life without growth does not exist. Stagnation leads to decay and death. Life adheres to these rules, and even though growth may be of almost imperceptible increments, as long as it abides it defies the power of death. Few are the creatures that grow in more than physical terms. Though one of the few, it remains rare that man, who has been granted limitless potential for mental, emotional, and spiritual growth, ever realizes that potential. Abundant life without prolific growth is, therefore, not possible. Yet forces around us contrive to dwarf our growth and strangle even our propensity to grow. I sometimes think I would surrender all I know to be released from the conventional tendencies that stunt growth. Often I resent what I have acquired, education, social station and physical security, for they have in reality acquired me. So out here, alone, I turn inward and try to nurture growth within my own being."

She snuggled deeper into his embrace. "Is that unlike the deep, intuitive penetration Bernard spoke of?" questioned Héloïse.

Abelard was ruffled a bit by her implication, "The difference remains that he merely accepts things, and I try to understand things."

"Faith versus reason, irreconcilable partners in their mutual search for truth," rejoined Héloïse.

Abelard was a little bewildered by this person he had thought to be an ally. He loosened his arms from around her. "You think not the struggle to discover truth by the questing and thirsting after knowledge, the use of all our faculties of mind and senses, is as profound, even as honourable, as relinquishing oneself of the struggle by merely believing?"

"You fight against not knowing; they surrender to not knowing."

Still debating, Abelard went on, "But these men of faith will not even acknowledge that reason could be an avenue to discovering truth and the nature of God. They consider it perverse and vile."

"And arrogant reason views faith as naïve," countered Héloïse. "The point is that we should all, at least, choose what we believe, and choose the way we arrive at those beliefs, instead of just letting it be by happenstance, instead of just being told what to believe." She pulled his arms back around her like a cosy blanket.

"Yes. You are a cunning creature," remarked Abelard. "Let us not be victims of circumstances, but victors over our own destinies."

"Agreed," affirmed Héloïse. "Of that I pledge." Then looking skyward again, Héloïse observed, "Some people believe that the stars are really the spirits of special persons who have passed away from the earth and now keep watch on us from above. Their light continues to shine as a reminder to live as they have lived, boldly, honourably, with compassion and love. Do you think we will get to be stars?" she enquired of Abelard while nestling peacefully into his arms.

"You will be the brightest of them all," he assured her.

Someone who sparks growth in a person is endeared by Abelard. He has told me they are "rare and precious." He says they are like the sun, and that whoever basks in their life-generating energy will produce much fruit. He says it is wise to search these people out and, once finding them, stay close to them. They may be discovered through intimate conversation or, perhaps, by gentle touch or warm embrace. I think this stimulation he calls "growth" can be more precisely understood as desire or romance, or perhaps love, depending upon the level of physical or mental involvement attached to the perception.

After an extended conversation in the woods, the two of them finally returned to camp. John and the rest of the men had long gone to sleep and had let the fire burn low. Abelard rebuilt the fire and laid himself on the ground. He propped his back up against a log close to the fire. Héloïse positioned herself next to him and watched the fire until drowsiness invaded her mind and her head felt heavy with sleep, and she rested it on Abelard's chest. "You must write it all down," Héloïse said with a yawn.

"What?" asked Abelard quietly.

"You must write down all the things you said to me this night," she replied. "You must write down all your thoughts. They are not meant for my ears alone."

"I did not choose the life of a scribe," complained Abelard. "Besides, it was the *word* of the Lord, not the letters that had the power to change the world and the way people perceived it."

"And your words are inspired and powerful, also," she asserted. "Further, had not Matthew, Mark, Luke, and John written them down, Christ's word would have never been able to reach us through the barrier of time."

"Yes, but the writing down of the word, especially the re-writing of it over time, often corrupts its original intent and meaning."

"All the more reason for the orator to be the author," argued Héloïse, "So there can be no misinterpretation." She relaxed her head more completely upon Abelard's bosom and said, "Before I sleep, a promise make, that you will faithfully write down your thoughts and words, for they will serve as guidance to others, a source of counsel and comfort for generations to come. Not unlike the Holy Spirit that God has sent us, will your word remain with those who allow it entry into their hearts and minds. And, as part of this promise, whatever we do, however far life may separate us, always write to me."

The last part of Héloïse's appeal so touched Abelard that he could not refuse the oath she requested, "For you, sweet Héloïse, I will write. For you and to you will I scribe my thoughts and dreams, but I think no other will ever read my words with as sympathetic eyes as yours."

She rolled her head up Abelard's chest to look into his face and smiled, then turned it away to fall asleep contentedly in his embrace.

In the morning Héloïse woke to find John and Abelard already up and preparing break-fast over the fire. The others began stirring from their slumber at the smell of fresh cooked eggs. "Where did you find those eggs?" Héloïse wondered aloud.

"There's a farm not too far from here," said John, "With a henhouse ripe for a stealthy fox's midnight raid."

"A two-legged fox, I do not doubt," chided Héloïse.

John just laughed. During break-fast one of the students mentioned that they should get an early start in order to return to Paris in time to meet Fulbert at the appointed hour. Abelard did not seem to be in a hurry. Abelard was older than it was usual for a student to be. He had not sought the ecclesiastical advancement to which most of his peers had aspired. He was an accomplished scholastic, much better educated than the majority of his teachers, and was well known for his debating skills and songs. He was allowed to lecture students, even though he was not a master. However, he never became even remotely interested in further involvement with the politics of the Church. Most likely that was because he knew he had committed too many political faux pas in the past by what he had said and now, from this time forward because of his promise to Héloïse, by what he would subsequently write.

"Perhaps we should make our way," said Abelard finally, and everyone rose to their feet to set off for the city.

Abelard's infatuation with the flowery countenance of Mother Nature continued. He again pointed out the golden meadow and purple banks of the river as the troupe approached their destination. They had to make a swift trip in order to be on time for Fulbert's scheduled lecture that afternoon, but they laughed and sang most of the way under Abelard's direction.

My group arrived early for the canon's lecture. It had only taken an hour or two for us to accomplish our mission, not a day or two. Lotulpt and I waited impatiently for Fulbert's arrival. When he had come, Lotulpt complained bitterly about the tardiness of Abelard's group. "Who does he think he is," snipped Lotulpt to those who had gathered, "To keep Canon Fulbert waiting for him?" He then whispered to me, "I would venture to say the female slowed Abelard down. And who could blame him for the delay? Who would want to return such a pleasure as she must be?"

"Here they are," said one of the students after spotting Abelard's group not far away.

John, Abelard, and Héloïse were almost sprinting now, as if racing, to meet up with the rest of us. They stopped directly in front of Fulbert, but bent over to try and catch their breath while laughing at the same time. Finally, Abelard stood up and acted more solemn. "My deepest apologies, Fulbert, for being so tardy; it is entirely my fault."

"It usually is!" replied the schoolmaster who seemed to take no offence at their levity or lateness. "Well, yellow-beaks, before my lecture, tell me about the results of the missions on which I sent you."

Fulbert often called his students "yellow-beaks" because he likened them to baby birds with bright yellow beaks and mouths wide open to eagerly receive whatever sustenance was forthcoming. Abelard said it meant that we students have to take whatever is shoved down our throats.

"Alberic, you go first," said Fulbert.

I was a little embarrassed by the menial task Fulbert had given my group, but I was determined to make the most of it for my schoolmaster's sake.

"Dear Fulbert," I began, "You charged me and my group to roam the countryside to see if there were any weeds growing up this spring." I really expected to hear laughter from Abelard and his group after I announced my assignment, but there was none. "I am sorry to report that weeds are growing in profusion, being found everywhere in gardens, along the pathways, and from the very cracks in the cobblestone streets. They are prevalent within the city walls and throughout the fields to such an extent I wonder if this pandemic can ever be stopped!" Perhaps I was slightly dramatic, but I thought I knew what Fulbert was expecting from my report. The weeds must surely have been symbolic of the wickedness and evil that invades the entire world.

Without comment, Fulbert turned to Abelard and said, "Let's hear from your group."

"Well," began John, "I do not know what we were actually supposed to do during this mission on which you sent us, but I can tell you that Alberic is absolutely wrong! I did not see any weeds in our travels."

Héloïse piped in, "In fact the countryside is fresh with the sweet smell of flowers and they cover the hills and roadside in resplendent colours."

Another from Abelard's group came forward to respond. "In the city, flowers have been cultivated by careful hands to produce beautiful gardens that delight our senses."

"And God's creative hand is everywhere throughout nature to gladden our souls by its beauty," responded another.

Fulbert was quiet for a moment and then remarked, "I guess one sees what one is seeking." Fulbert had just been mingling among us up until then. He moved through the class to take his place upon the rock that had become his personal pulpit. "As lovers of Christ, we should know what we are seeking. That is to see goodness in others and His world. Christians are to be optimists, not pessimists. And how do we become an optimist? …By simply choosing to see the pleasant sights over ugliness, the delightful over the unsightly, and by maintaining a kindness of mind that discards malice." Fulbert turned in the direction of Lotulpt and me. "Christians should motivate and inspire others. Jesus was a great optimist and He brought out the best in everyone He touched. Such is the example we are to follow."

Chapter Eight

The Love Letter

O sun, I cannot escape you! I cannot live in the shadows or darkness.

The teaching and learning sessions began as scheduled between Abelard and Héloïse, but it was difficult at times to know who was teaching and who was learning. Héloïse had a mind of her own and was not afraid to speak it. As far as Abelard was concerned this was an admirable quality and he seemed fascinated that it was being displayed in such an appealing form – that of a beautiful maiden.

This day I had been invited to join the two at Fulbert's house for Héloïse's tutoring. Abelard had urged me to go with him. The two had been meeting privately during the past few weeks on a more-than-necessary basis in the opinion of many. My hunch was that my accompanying him to Fulbert's house was to allay suspicions that the teaching sessions had become more intimate than appropriate and that my presence would make it appear to be a chaperoned and respectable affair.

Abelard's step was light and quick as we made our way to Fulbert's house. He had little to say to me. In fact, I could see by the sparkle in his eyes that his mind was preoccupied with thoughts that were inciting deep emotions within him. This was the same distant stare he displayed when delivering an impassioned plea for a favourite cause or idea. I recognized it well.

Héloïse was at her threshold as we approached Fulbert's house. Abelard rushed ahead of me and said something quietly to Héloïse before I reached the door. "Is Master Fulbert gone," Abelard asked.

"Yes," answered Héloïse, "We are alone."

"Well, not exactly," said Abelard as he patted me hard on the shoulder. "I brought along our dear friend."

"Oh," replied Héloïse while never taking her eyes off Abelard. "Hello, Alberic."

"Hello," was all the conversation I could muster. Héloïse was spellbinding. She turned and escorted us into the house with graceful movement and flair. Héloïse exhibited uniqueness among women by her strong sense of freedom to express herself, not just through words, but also through her body language. Her gestures were expansive and open, always welcoming. She would touch the person with whom she was talking. She would touch her self, such as by placing a hand across her bosom to demonstrate emotion or running a finger across her lips when she listened intently. She would let down her hair among friends, as it was this day.

"What are you studying today?" I asked innocently since there seemed to be no manuscripts set out for study.

"Sometimes, we may just sit and talk," quickly answered Abelard while Héloïse nodded affirmatively. "Here, sit, and join in our discussions."

We all sat at Fulbert's strong wooden table that was used for multiple purposes, to eat upon, to work on, as a desk, and now as an implement conducive to conversation. Abelard and Héloïse positioned themselves across from each other at the table while I sat at one end of it. I could almost imagine, at the opposite end of the table, which was its head, Fulbert sitting at his normal place.

The two were locked into each other's gaze until I interrupted them by asking, "What shall we talk about?"

This time Héloïse was quick to respond, "We had been discussing people in general, how they feel, how they live, and what brings meaning to their lives."

"Yes," agreed Abelard. "We believe that society is changing, that the Church needs to be aware of those changes and find ways to remain important to people."

"At one time," continued Héloïse, "All the Church had to offer the poor and downtrodden, which represented the majority of people, was the hope of a better life after this one. Now, with large classes of wealthier merchants and tradesmen, people are looking to find meaning in *this* life."

"But often they look for the wrong things in this life if they do not keep their eyes on Heaven," I cautioned.

"Exactly," said Abelard, "Men still have the tendency to serve themselves before they serve God. That is why the Church must not fail in reaching out to the people in new and exciting ways. And one way to accomplish this is to address their doubts, not subjugating them with guilt."

"You mean that people should not feel guilty for their sins, or for the death of Christ upon the cross?" I asked, almost horrified at the thought that any Christian would not experience such pain.

"You have heard it said that sin is in the eye of the beholder," began Abelard. "You and I both believe that is not an appropriate tenet of our faith. But, sin is judged with the eye of God, and that can frequently be different than sin seen through the eyes of man. Christ did not die because of our sin. He did not intend to have us live under the guilt of his death. His sacrifice enables us to live saved and forgiven through him. I believe that human actions do not make a man better or worse in the sight of God, for deeds themselves are neither good nor bad. What counts are a man's intentions; sin is not something done, it is uniquely the consent of a human mind to do what it knows is wrong."

"Lotulpt recently commented to me that people's attitudes have certainly changed in these parts," I remarked. "It seems that sin is being defined differently or conveniently to suit a particular situation."

"Lotulpt is no more than Bernard's mole!" piped in Héloïse, "Turning up dirt to find some juicy morsel on which to chew. I would be careful what you tell him, Alberic, because he will use it against you."

"He would use it against us all," warned Abelard. "Perhaps we should call an early end to this session today."

"But we never discussed doubts," I complained.

"There will be opportunities for that," replied Abelard. He gently took Héloïse's hand and with a smile rose to his feet to leave. Héloïse returned the smile and clutched his hand eagerly to delay his departure if only for a brief moment. Without another word we left. Outside the door Abelard stated, "You and I need to talk, alone, at my place, late tonight. Be there." He took off without waiting for my reply.

I meandered around the area for a while thinking about returning to Fulbert's house to see Héloïse on my own. As I had almost summoned up enough courage to do so, I received a surprise slap on the back.

"Alberic, ole friend," hailed Lotulpt. "What do you know today?"

Taken aback by his unexpected appearance, "Lotulpt!" I stammered, "I … uh … do not know anything."

"Well you'll let me know if you ever do, won't you?" responded Lotulpt with a wink before he continued on his way.

"Sure," I replied, still feeling a little bewildered by all the things that had just happened. I felt some explanation was due me about Abelard and Héloïse's comments concerning Lotulpt, so that would be rationale enough to return to talk alone with Héloïse. With raised fist poised at her door, I, alas, could not bring myself to complete the simple procedure that would bring her to me. Perhaps, because I did not knock, all ensuing misfortunes were on my hands.

The spring had brought with it longer days. When Abelard had told me to see him late this night I presumed he meant after dark at least. So I tarried along the Seine and looked for the purple patches of heartsease to which Abelard and Héloïse had alluded, but found the blossoms had all withered or dropped from the plants, leaving only a carpet of green that was indistinguishable from the other grasses and weeds.

As darkness finally set in, I decided to cross the river via the sole causeway that connected the central city island to its expansion on the south bank of the Seine. The Romans had made Paris a regional capital almost a thousand years earlier and left this ancient construction of now weathered limestone arches and smoothly worn paving stones as a testament to their great architectural skills. It seemed that nearly the entire population of Paris would pass over the bridge each day. The residents along the southern bank of the Seine would pilgrimage to the heart of the city, and those on the island would travel out to enjoy the spaciousness of the countryside. Even if there was no purpose in their crossing, some would walk on the bridge merely to be seen and to socialize with other fellow sojourners. This expanse of stone was the city's lifeline, not only for the transportation of necessary survival goods or daily staples, but also for the transmission of information vital to the solidifying of the civil society.

After reaching the southwest end of the bridge, I headed to a large old building that had been divided up into smaller dwellings for individual inhabitants. The building may once have served to garrison soldiers who would have monitored the outermost perimeter walls of the ancient city. Over the years, the burgeoning population of Paris had burst these walls open, and now the bridge was patrolled by only a token guard whose job it was to greet, in the name of the King, those who freely passed over it.

Abelard lived in this old building and his apartment was small and sparsely furnished. A writing easel was the room's most prominent fixture and around it were manuscripts, both old and freshly penned. There was no evidence of overindulgence or excessive attention to personal ease. The luxury of the place was the fact that it was a distance from the university housing that was even more confined and less private. Most students were not even afforded the meagre comforts that Abelard enjoyed. The focal point of the room was a large window that framed a view of the city beyond the Seine. Abelard's seat at the easel was positioned so that he could keep one eye on this scene at all times.

As a welcomed and habitual guest, I only knocked once upon Abelard's door before letting myself in. He was at his easel, finishing up a note on a small piece of paper. "Ah, Alberic, just in time," he said to acknowledge my arrival. "Like the fine wooden body of the lute, be my sounding board and tell me if this will convey the message I desire to one whom I hope reads it with sympathetic eyes." He began to read.

> *"A fertile garden lies within each of us that is capable of producing abundant life, but it cannot cultivate itself. No garden can grow without other essential elements; the seed, the soil, the rain, and the sun.*
> *The seed is within us; what we are by the Creator's hand. The soil is what we put ourselves into; what we have come to believe and hold dear. The rain is our experiences, sometimes gentle and other times torrential, but nonetheless life-enriching. And, the sun is the light that inspires us all to grow and live. And, while the sun's life-generating energy is indiscriminately spread upon all the gardens, it brings forth fruit only to those willing to bask in its radiance. O sun, I cannot escape you! I cannot live in the shadows or darkness. Full-face I look upon you and bare myself to your mighty power. In my exposure your rays can strike me down or sustain me, but in either event I confess my uttermost dependence upon you."*

I had to interrupt him. "Is this a witness to Ra?" I said facetiously.

"Of course not," Abelard said in a serious tone. "You and I both know there is but one Son worthy of our devotion and dedication, and that He is love incarnate. That is the essential and greatest power of which I speak. But, let me finish," he asserted, and he began to read again.

> *"You are like the sun, radiant and warm, exuding energy and light, and encouraging life to grow out from the basest soil. And, like the sun, you have no pretence to reserve your radiance for the few, but*

have enough to share with all. And that is why I do not know how the sun reacts to my worship. Is it flattered or oblivious? Sweet Héloïse, how do you bear such devotion?"

"Héloïse," I said in a startled voice, "This is about Héloïse?"

"Yes, dear confidant, I cannot contain my feelings for her. All my thoughts are spent on her. All my actions revolve around our next meeting. I am held captive by her, but I am a willing prisoner."

"Does she know how you feel?" I asked.

"She will, without question, when you deliver this to her," he replied. Abelard folded up the letter with sharp creases and held it forth for my acceptance. "Please," he added to his request.

At first, I did not accept his delegation. "How do you think she will receive this?" I wondered aloud.

"The way she looks at me and the way she freely lays a hand upon me betrays her innermost feelings," Abelard explained.

"But she does that to all her friends, even me," I explained.

"Of course," he said, as he looked me directly in the eyes, "Because you are very special to her, too."

"You cannot marry her, you will only bring shame upon her! You would have to abandon all possibilities for your ecclesiastical advancement. She would not allow it for your sake, nor should you for hers."

Putting his hand upon my shoulder he said, "I have dispelled all doubts about my love for her."

My doubts remained. "You are twenty years her elder and should recognize the difference between love and lust," I argued. "Of course, her beauty is beckoning, and your desire is keen for her such as it would be in any man. But she is the niece of Canon Fulbert, not some street wench with whom you can have your way without consequence."

"The consequences may be severe, but the consequences of not loving her would be more severe." Then quietly he added, "It is something that I did not choose or seek out, but have come to accept as part of my life's journey whether it be ordained or of human origin. If serious consequences arise, those, too, become part of my journey to take in stride on the way to my final destination."

Abelard presented me the letter again, "Tomorrow?" he asked.

Taking the paper from his hand, I said, "I am not convinced. Man plays games with the Fates' spinning, but often finds too late the only thread left dangling on which to hang is the one attached to God." Then I turned to leave. "I am compromised by doing this," I said while holding the letter high in the air as I departed.

"Hurry back," Abelard called to me, "And bring me her response."

"I will most certainly do that!" I exclaimed, "For she will have none of this!"

Abelard may have said something after that, but I was already too far away to hear it. It was late and I was ready to return to the solace of my room at the university. Beginning my trek across the bridge, I deposited Abelard's letter into my cloak and withdrew another that had been previously secreted there. Then, at the midway point of the bridge, a vantage point from which the approach of someone from either side could be detected early, I read to myself the second one.

> *"I started writing this missal for what seems to be a long time ago. Perhaps I have been composing it my whole life. The words do not flow easily, not because of insincere emotions, but because of the quality of expression I wish to extend to you and the breadth of understanding I hope to receive. My anticipation accelerates, as does my apprehension, when I think of you reading this. It is meant for a heart of which I am unsure. But time is a villain and I dare not delay, for it moves so stealthily and swiftly and leaves me empty each time it defeats me. All that should be done and said is not done nor said during time's perpetual victory over me. If only I could win a brief battle against it, if not by being in your arms, by being in your thoughts. But I am resolved that my identity must remain forever hidden, for I can expect nothing favourable from destiny in the matters of love. Yet I do not apologize for my feelings, only do I apologize if their expression proves offensive, for I have no right to impose them upon you."*

Refolding the letter, I returned it to its safe place and finished the long and lonely walk across the bridge, past the watchman, and onto the university grounds – only there could I find rest and serenity away from the daily clanging of the outside world and the madness that besets men.

When the next morn arrived, it presented me with the dilemma of which letter I should deliver – the one in my charge or the one that is the charge of my heart. Or should I deliver both and let Héloïse's response determine what course was correct? Assessing the possibilities, without question Héloïse would know the author of one, but I being the bearer of my own anonymous letter might help further the deception. Or would it make it obvious! I am no good at conniving, and, as I approached Fulbert's house, I bore each letter in a separate hand unsure of whether the right or left would be presented to the unsuspecting recipient.

Standing by, some distance away from the house, I waited until Fulbert had set out for his usual morning activities. Fulbert's routine was disciplined and orderly. He varied little from his daily rituals. One could count on where he would be and when he would be there, but one could never be completely sure of what he was thinking.

I started toward the house to make the delivery, my heart pounding so hard that beads of sweat began streaming down my brow like a man with the fever. The closer I came to the door, the more ill I became, first with uncontrollable shakes, followed by nausea. Arriving at the point of no return, the door of Fulbert's abode, a decision had to be made – the right or the left, the left or the right. Oh, if thy hand offends thee, cut it off!

I stood there frozen, like a gargoyle keeping watch over a house of worship, and I probably looked as grotesque, too, for my face was surely contorted by its expression of all the suffering coursing inside me. I could not move. I could not knock. I could not speak aloud to call upon her name. I could hardly breathe.

Then, in a panic, I thrust one letter halfway through the crack between the door and threshold, and tore the other into pieces small enough that my clenched hand could conceal it completely. Gasping for breath, I ran from the place until I reached the edge of the river, and tossed the mutilated page far into the air. The pieces spread out through the breeze and floated listlessly down toward the perpetual flow of water. I wished for an acceleration to the watery end of those cryptic words, but as they met the surface of the slowly moving Seine, they seemed to form together again into the whole as they drifted off.

My panic resurfaced, for what if those soggy fragments were fished ashore and my fait accompli uncovered? Running along the bank, I picked up stone after stone and hurled them at the floating target in hopes of breaking it asunder again. The ripples from many near misses began to disperse the pieces once more, until, at last, with a loud gulp, a direct hit by a large rock forced down the bulk of the shattered document to the river's muddy bottom.

Plopping on the ground in exhaustion, I closed my eyes to try to relieve my dizziness. Opening them again to the sky above, my vision was filled with the majesty of billowing clouds as they paraded across the field of blue, indifferent to what was happening below.

My calmed mood was soon interrupted by the thought that Abelard expected me to report on how Héloïse had responded to his letter. What was I to do? How could I feign an answer without giving away what I had done? I resolved that what I must do was to return to Fulbert's house and finish my commission. I would retrieve the letter from under the door and present it properly, and, for my sake as well as Abelard's, find out her reaction and relay it to him. However, upon my return, I discovered that the letter was no longer halfway in and halfway out of the slot beneath the door, but was gone. How could I now face Héloïse without looking like a coward?

I moved stealthily around to the back of the house to Héloïse's window. She had an unobstructed view of the

Seine, which was only at a distance of some one hundred yards away. Fulbert's garden was well kept, with rows of fresh vegetables for physical sustenance and carefully laid-out flowering landscaping for spiritual sustenance. Then, in what must be considered a fortuitous and timely happenstance, while standing behind one of the larger bushes in the garden, I spotted Héloïse coming into her room and reading the letter I had previously delivered. From this concealed location I could see a new pallor coming over her face and the welling up of tears in her eyes. When she reached the end of the letter, Héloïse dove to her bed and issued wails of despair into her pillow.

I could watch no more. I ran again from the house, ill now from the anguish I must have brought her! How could I expect acceptance of this expression of base and worldly love from one so pure and innocent? My wondering and wanderings continued throughout the day. I crossed back and forth over the city's bridge many times, first one way to report to Abelard, then one way to reconcile things with Héloïse, but never reaching either destination. As the evening approached, I knew I had no choice but to face Abelard and his inevitable questions about my mission. What should I tell him? ...The truth?

Each time, my unconscious wanderings to and fro had brought me closer and closer to Abelard's house before I awoke and turned the other way. Once, though, he finally noticed my coming and yelled out, "Alberic, where have you been all day?"

Reluctantly completing the distance to his house, I said, "I have had much to do today," but I blushed at the inaccuracy of that statement.

"Come in, come in," prodded Abelard as he ushered me through his doorway. "What news?" Abelard left me standing while he sat upon the wooden stool next to his easel and directed his full attention to what I was about to say. He waited in silence until he finally must have felt it necessary to prompt me by asking, "How did she respond?"

"Not well, not well at all," I told him, "She turned pale and wept in anguish."

"What, then, did you say to her?" he asked in disbelief.

"Nothing, Abelard, what would you have me say?" I retorted. "I left immediately so as to not prolong her discomfort."

"Oh, Alberic, I am sorry for your trouble. I had expected that you would be able to share in the joy of my love's revelation, but you could not. I should not have asked it of you. Forgive me, you have been a good friend." Then Abelard jumped up to his feet and pronounced with determination, "Tonight, I will go to her as I should have done, and plead love's case."

"Should you do so?" I questioned. "Would this not irritate an already sensitive wound?"

"If she is wounded, then I shall be the salve, for in my heart I know that love heals, not injures."

"You should not do this," I warned. "A secret meeting between you two, found out, would have serious repercussions."

"Then I will go to her now, while all are awake, and make my love known."

"No, no, you cannot do that," I begged. "Remember such an affirmation may bring scorn upon Héloïse even in her innocence. Wait a few hours, during the darkest night, if you dare go to her. You must avoid the watchman on the bridge for he tells everything about the goings on at night to whoever will listen. Take care." With that warning, I left.

My words, I hoped, would discourage any attempt by Abelard to see Héloïse for at least the night. He could not cross over the bridge to the city without being seen, and that would certainly put Héloïse in jeopardy. Fulbert might lock her up or send her away to a nunnery. But, just in case, that night I took my station behind the same bush in the garden that had hid my presence before, to keep watch of the bridge for travellers from the south who might be bent on invading the sanctity of Fulbert's house.

The night wore on with no sign of trouble. My head nodded in drowsiness and, because of my complacency that all had gone as expected, complete relaxation and eventually slumber set in. At one of those times between sleep and consciousness, I looked out upon the Seine and caught a glimpse of something in the river. It was a figure swimming the great expanse of water toward the island city. The swimmer moved silently and steadily closer to shore. My first suspicions were correct that it was Abelard. His lanky limbs sliced smoothly through the water. What he was doing was no mean feat, for from his starting point he would have to swim more than half a mile to reach his objective in a river not yet warmed by the summer sun.

Watching his progress, I marvelled at his determined stroke, never faltering, never resting, he made his way across the river, until, at last, he pulled himself upon the bank. Without even catching a breath, he crept quietly across the three hundred feet of open field to Fulbert's house. When should I intercept this trespasser? ... Before or after he commits a crime? Abelard was approaching rapidly. I decided to wait.

Now at the window Abelard paused long enough to wring out his clothes and comb back his dripping locks with his fingers before whispering, "Héloïse."

Rushing to the window from the other side came Héloïse. "I knew you would come tonight," she whispered in return.

"I came to apologize if my letter caused you distress," said Abelard.

She reached across the sill and flung her arms around his neck. "Oh, Abelard, I cried for joy when I read your words and was overcome with relief that you felt as I do."

"Then you are not disturbed by my affirmation of love?" he asked in a perplexed tone.

"You are more than the mere sun to me, but also the moon, and the stars, and the entire universe. You are my all." Then, with a kiss, she drew him all the way through the window and murmured, "Come, tend your garden."

Chapter Nine

Treachery

*N*othing!" *I cried, "Nothing! I want to know nothing!"*

The late night rendezvous continued into the summer. To avoid suspicion, the two would meet publicly less and less. It had almost reached the point where Abelard only came to visit Héloïse during the day at Fulbert's explicit request.

Fulbert also extended invitations to his home to me and I readily accepted them. However much of our discussion centred on Abelard, with Fulbert almost always defending Abelard's position on things; he felt that Bernard disliked Abelard's humanism and "mistook Abelard's intellectualism for derogation from the obedience of faith."

Anyway, I was glad to spend time with him and Héloïse even though she seemed distant and languid and he regularly retold the same stories. She rarely took part in the conversation and might rudely doze off. Fulbert would then sometimes divulge to me an iota of information about his obscure past. Often, especially when he became overly tired, he would reminisce about a maiden he once knew. At those times, he would eat of that peculiar fruit and say how, "She introduced me to this life-giving food as she introduced me to life itself.

As this fruit her father traded for when he travelled south to Valencia refreshes my body, did she renew my weakened spirit." I thought it a bit unseemly that this pious man talked so affectionately about this maiden from his past.

But, I knew what was going on behind Fulbert's back. Héloïse had become nocturnal, a creature of the night. The day was merely time to pass until the anxiously anticipated darkness arrived to stir her into activity. How did I know this? It was because several times I, too, was awake at night watching Abelard's swim across the Seine to visit his secret love, watching him climb through her window, and hearing the muffled sounds of their fornication. No one else knew what I knew.

Unlike Héloïse, the daytime hours were not wasted by Abelard. He became reenergized in his writing and lecturing. One day, while I was visiting him in his apartment, John arrived with two guests.

"John!" greeted Abelard as he gave him a strong embrace.

"Abelard," John replied excitedly. "I want you to meet Peter Lombard Berenger and Arnold of Brescia, two apt and eager students." Then addressing the guests he had just announced, "Friends, this is Abelard, our imperial paladin."

Abelard shook the visitors' hands and said, "I blush at John's introduction. It is more flattering than warranted. What is the purpose of your visit?" he asked politely.

John chimed in, "They have come to seek out a great teacher."

"Who might that be?" I asked of John.

"Why, Abelard, of course!" he answered while putting his arm across Abelard's shoulder. "His writings are gaining him great repute all over France. Students come from far and wide to hear him speak. These two are among the most promising young scholastics of the day, and they want to work under Abelard's guidance."

"That is again flattering, John," Abelard responded, then turning to his guests he said, "I am sorry John has filled you with hopes that cannot be fulfilled. The thoughts expressed in my writings and lectures are in sharp contrast with those of power in the Church. It would not be fair to enjoin you with them and the trouble they may bring to fruition."

"We fully understand that," replied Peter, "And we are prepared to follow your teaching wherever it might lead."

"Your namesake once professed a similar determination, but was unable to follow through on his pledge," admonished Abelard.

"We will not shirk conflict," assured Arnold.

John was still enthusiastic, "It is time for the university to move to the south bank of the Seine; time for it to expand physically and intellectually." Looking around the room and raising his arms, he spoke on, "What better place to house it than in an ancient army barracks. It is war, war of words versus wisdom, and there may be casualties."

"John, will you be there when they hang me from a tree?" Abelard asked quietly.

"Yes, gladly," John laughed.

"I believe you would be," said Abelard with a big smile, "Hopefully right alongside of me."

"Then you will consent to having these two become the start of your new league of students?" John asked as he escorted them closer to Abelard.

I am sure I saw Abelard glance my way when he said, "Let me give it further thought."

Appalled by what I was hearing, the near treason being expressed by those I respected, I felt I should go and leave them to their plotting, but John acquiesced first. "All right," he said. "I'm disappointed, but I'll overcome it. And, do not think that I have given up. These two would be a fine legacy to your teaching. We will talk again."

After cordial goodbyes, John and the students left the apartment. "Well, what do you think?" asked Abelard.

What did I think? Abelard knew very well what I was thinking, but I played along with his game. "What do you mean," I asked coyly.

"What do you think about what was discussed here? Do you agree with John that it is time to challenge the university's teachings in a more organized and deliberate way, even to the point of establishing a competing school of thoughts?"

"I think the Church's tenets are indisputable. For a thousand years they have been handed down in a direct line from our Lord, Jesus Christ, through Peter, His Disciple and our first Bishop of Rome. Our faithful adherence to God's rules has been a successful way of life for centuries. Why question our creed if we call ourselves Christians? It is what Christians are to believe. If we do not believe what the Church says, then we should have a different label."

"Now, tell me what you really believe," he said. "Tell me how you feel about friendship, and love, and life, and God, and how they all mix together. Tell me how the majestic spires and glittering altars of the Church soothes a hungry baby's cry, or how the cold confessional replaces the warm embrace of a friend, or how a life of solitude has more spiritual dignity than a life shared by two."

"I cannot tell you how I feel," I cried. "Sometimes I do not think I know. Maybe I'm still searching. You are so sure. I am not. Can you help me?"

Abelard came to my side and softly said, "I love you, Alberic."

Overcome, I kissed his cheek, and with eyes full of tears, I ran from his house, his embrace, his care.

On my way back from the southern bank, I met Lotulpt just as I entered the city. He quickly came up to me and glared into my face. "Do you know what your friend is conspiring to do?" he asked accusingly. "Rumours are that he is establishing himself as the head of his own school. Students are flocking to him and even some in our own ranks are deserting to his way of thinking. Bernard is furious! Have you gone over to the other side as well?"

Trying to soothe his temper, "I think the rumours presume too much," I replied. "Abelard has made no such plans to my knowledge."

"Abelard portrays the reluctant hero who rises to an occasion that seems beyond other men's control, but, in reality, he is the creator of those circumstances and should be held accountable, not in awe. He is a rabble-rouser and rebel."

"That may be a bit too strong," I argued.

"Do you think so?" said Lotulpt in a louder voice. "Have you read his work, *Sic et Non*, where he reduces religion to the whim of man by suggesting he has the right to say yes or no to any tenet of the Church?"

"I think Abelard's manuscript was written to sharpen the wits of young students, and not as a great theological argument. Its intent was more to say that it is acceptable to question the validity of any idea. You and I have both felt restricted in our freedom to query, to doubt . . ."

"Not I, dear Alberic, not I," asserted Lotulpt. "My faith is sure and founded in the Church."

"Abelard is as an explorer without maps. He is in uncharted territory, nothing more. Leave him there and he will soon be lost."

"But how many more will be lost with him?" Lotulpt countered. "Bernard wants Abelard stopped now. If you are not for us, you are against us, there is no middle ground when it comes to serving God!"

"I am not against you, but I am not against Abelard either, except for some personal matters."

"What personal matters?" questioned Lotulpt with great interest. "Do you, as I, wonder how such a righteous man can carry on personally the way he does?"

Turning away from him, I answered, "I do not know what you mean."

"Sure you do," coaxed Lotulpt as he stepped round to face me once again. "You know much more than what you are saying. I'll bet this has something to do with Fulbert's niece. It is shameful the way Abelard has been acting toward her, compromising her virtue, you see."

I did not react to his implications.

"That body of hers probably quells a man's fire well," he continued. "Such womanly anatomy is hard to resist. I doubt many of us would push it aside if it were thrust upon us, eh Alberic?"

I did not know in whose defence to respond, Abelard's, Héloïse's, or my own, so I remained silent.

Stalking around me like a wolf sniffing his prey, Lotulpt went on, "You know, I always believed those lessons were more tryst than tutoring. But, they have stopped and there is no evidence of that. I confess, for a while, I watched the coming and going of Abelard at Fulbert's house. I would stand at the windows and listen to their conversations. As you would be, if necessary I was ready to defend Héloïse's honour, and the honour of Fulbert's house, if Abelard made an improper advance upon her. Thankfully, while I watched, nothing happened."

"Then you have not watched closely enough," I said through clenched teeth.

Lotulpt's pacing and tirade suddenly stopped. "Well, good day, Alberic, and thank you." He took off toward the university. I pretended to go off in the direction of Fulbert's house. When I was certain that Lotulpt could not detect my true destination, I hurried back across the bridge to Abelard's house.

Bursting through his doorway, all out of breath, I asked the startled Abelard, "Why do you no longer speak to me of Héloïse?"

"I did not think there was anything you wanted to hear," he answered calmly. "I longed to tell you of our joy and happiness. What do you want to know?"

"Nothing!" I cried, "Nothing! I want to know nothing!" Abelard came up to me and I grabbed his arms. "Stop what you are doing," I implored him. "Do not go to her tonight. Do not go to her ever again."

"What you are asking of me is impossible," he replied.

"No it is not," I pleaded, "For the love of God, do not go to Héloïse!"

"For the love of Héloïse, I must," he countered.

Releasing his arms from my grasp, "Then do what you must," I said, "But the consequences are upon your shoulders not mine." Waiting for no other word from him, I left.

Heading once again back to the centre of the city, I devised a scheme that might help Abelard avert the dire circumstances awaiting him. I would go to Fulbert's house and stay there late. Maybe I would get invited to stay overnight if I could engage Fulbert with conversation that continued far into the wee hours of the morning. As long as a light was lit in the house, Abelard would certainly hesitate to call on Héloïse. Better yet, maybe I could persuade her to stay up with us passed her contrived bedtime so that she would be absent from any raid upon their illicit affair.

Implementing my plan was more difficult than I expected. I spent the evening with Fulbert and Héloïse for a while, but he was tired and in no mood for idle conversation. Héloïse feigned fatigue, so the two of them insisted on my early departure. "Alberic, go home," Fulbert suggested, "It is late and we all need rest; come again another day." Of course I had to abide by his wishes, so I left.

Hardly any distance away from Fulbert's house, Lotulpt appeared from out of the darkness. "Want to stay and see if the trap is sprung?" he asked me.

"Not particularly," I replied.

Lotulpt grabbed hard my arm. "Well, do not interfere then," he warned.

"Why should I?" was my reply as I pulled loose from his grasp.

I walked off and thought that perhaps I should sneak back, climb through the window to waiting Héloïse, and tell her everything. If I was found with Héloïse, who would care? In fact, Lotulpt would be the laughingstock of the university if he managed only to capture me with Héloïse. His plan would be spoiled, and, by the spoiling of it, that would serve as a warning to Abelard of Lotulpt's malevolent intent.

However, after more serious consideration, I realized there was nothing I could do, so I decided to return to campus. Suddenly I received a hard jolt from the back. It was John. "Judas!" he growled.

"What?" I said, shoving him back.

"I watched you talking to Lotulpt," he snapped. "What did you tell him?"

"I do not know what you are talking about, John," I said as I started to walk away. Again I received a hard jolt from behind that jerked my shoulders back so quickly that a shot of hot pain went down my neck and spine. "What are you doing?" I exclaimed.

"I'm teaching a traitor a lesson," he snarled.

"What are you talking about?" I pleaded.

"You were talking to Lotulpt earlier this afternoon for quite awhile, and then again tonight. It seems the two of you are conspiring something."

"About what?" I asked.

"About Abelard, I suspect," he said with daggers in his eyes.

"Now, wait, wait, I told him nothing that he did not already know," I replied in an assuring way. "He asked about Abelard's teaching, what I thought of it, and whether he had begun teaching any students, to which I replied 'No.' After all, I was there with you when Abelard refused those students you brought him, so I was square with Lotulpt, too."

"What about Héloïse?" he asked suspiciously.

"Actually, Lotulpt made rude comments regarding her conduct, rather bawdy and lewd comments about her, for which I did not care. So I ended the conversation."

Calming down, John said, "We have to be careful with Lotulpt. He is out to get Abelard at any cost. And he would attack at the most personal level, not spar with Abelard's intellect or face him openly in scholarly debate."

"You mean in regards to him and Héloïse?" I asked.

"Yes, of course," answered John in a hushed voice. "Lotulpt only suspects, nothing more, but too little knowledge can still be dangerous. Even if he thinks he has proof, it may turn against him, for things are not always as they seem, are they?"

"No, you are right," I replied. "He really doesn't know the truth about Abelard and Héloïse, does he?"

Speaking in an even softer voice, John said, "No, he thinks they are living in sin. He doesn't know that Abelard presented Hymen to Héloïse, but that Héloïse would not publicly announce their marriage because it would compromise Abelard's position with the Church and university. Even that knowledge Lotulpt could use to his advantage, so we must guard it."

Married! Oh, what a deceitful pair – marrying to save a reputation, and denying it to save a career! Yet, they can't have both. He must either serve God as man or serve God as priest.

"You know, it is a little difficult to condone his actions, in Abelard's case, I mean," I said, thinking aloud. "St. Paul would have us lead a celibate life, to choose between masters, humanness or godliness."

"I asked Abelard about that and he explained it this way, 'Paul was a man, and like any man he had his personal biases. Some of that bias was toward women, and it is hard to imagine wherefrom that came. Christ did not show such bias, but then Paul never laid eyes on the Saviour, or sat next to Him, or heard his voice. Paul experienced a magnificent conversion and brought Christianity to the Gentiles, but his word is not law.'"

How could Abelard be so vain as to refute Paul, I thought.

"Abelard tries to live by Christ's great commandment instead, which was repeated to the early churches by the Apostle, John, to his dying day, to 'Love one another!'" Snidely the John in my presence added, "Besides, more despicable things than Abelard's love for Héloïse goes on behind the priest's closed door. How many of the most high and mighty of them could stand close scrutiny? Lotulpt himself? Bernard? Even Fulbert?"

Why should John know so much, I wondered? Am I not as much friend to Abelard? It might have lessened my grief and worry if Abelard or Héloïse had confided these things to me. Such treachery on both their parts to treat me so! "Well, I should go before Lotulpt sees us and thinks we're conspiring against him," I told John.

"Probably so," agreed John, and he took off into the darkness.

Everything was spinning around in my head. Perhaps it was because it was late, perhaps it was the jolts that I had received from John, but it was hard to think clearly anymore. Somehow, though, I felt relief, relief that they had made the fateful decision that would set the course to follow, not I. Héloïse was married, it was not my place to protect or defend her anymore, and Abelard's deeds would be left to the purview of the ever-vigilant Lotulpt.

It was an extremely dark night, probably a new moon, just the sort of night conducive to one of Abelard's secretive missions to see Héloïse. Completely exhausted, I could not think of travelling all the way back to my room, so I nestled beneath a sycamore tree far enough away from Fulbert's house that I would not be noticed, yet close enough to see any unusual activity.

Ever so slowly, two hours passed by before I caught sight of Abelard's figure in the water, a sight I had seen many times previously, but this time I watched with a heightened sense of excitement. I quietly climbed up into the tree to get a better look. I knew I was not the only pair of eyes peering into the darkness, and that caused a rush of energy throughout my body and increased my awareness of things happening around me. I noticed the croaking of the frogs along the bank of the river, a fish splashing the water as it broke the river's surface to snatch a flying insect, the light breeze bringing in the smell of rain from the west, and the almost imperceptible movement of men attempting to camouflage themselves in the darkness. When would Lotulpt strike? As Abelard pulls himself from the river, at Héloïse's window, or when he is in her arms?

In no time, Abelard reached the bank. Immediately, a second figure popped out of the tall grass. After a brief encounter, both disappeared from sight, and soon the swimmer was returning from whence he came. The interferer must have been John. Why did he tempt fate? Would not a true friend be merciful and let destiny have its inevitable way?

I slept under the tree that night until first light. Then I went to my room to sleep some more in order to recover from such a tiring evening of drained emotions and broken dreams.

Days passed and I busied myself with work that seemed to have been too long neglected. I studied and prayed, attended lectures, helped distribute bread to the poor, old, and ailing outside the city, went to confession, and celebrated the Eucharist. One chance evening I stopped to visit Fulbert.

Fulbert's welcome was warm as if he were receiving a long-lost friend. Héloïse had gone out to see friends with Thessaly who had recently arrived for a visit. In a short while, a loud pounding on the door interrupted our cordial conversation. It was Lotulpt accompanied by three other men whom I did not recognize. Lotulpt, only, stepped inside.

"Grave matters I bring to you, Fulbert," began Lotulpt.

"If they are matters of the grave, have at it, for death's messenger casts no fear in me." Fulbert paused briefly, and then added anxiously, "Unless the matter concerns my dear Héloïse."

"Were it as simple as that, for death may be a preferred substitute for what I am compelled to reveal." Lotulpt looked down and started to pace the floor.

"What is it, then?" asked Fulbert.

"Dear Canon, father to us all, it tears my heart out to have to tell you this. One whom you entrusted with your most valued treasure has betrayed you. He comes almost daily to her at night. Their fornication is widely known. I have witnessed his comings and goings with my own eyes as have others close to you." Lotulpt looked at me.

"Alberic, what do you know about this?" questioned Fulbert.

"I am just as shocked as you about this treachery," I replied.

Probably wanting to spare me any more discomfort, Lotulpt went on without further involving me, "He brings dishonour on this house, dishonour that can no longer be tolerated by those who revere you and feel you should be avenged."

"'Dishonour?' you may call it," said Fulbert. "Yet what is honourable? Vengeance? But I cannot convict him; 'Ye who is without sin cast the first stone.'"

Lotulpt was silent for a moment, and then turned to leave. I gave a hasty farewell to Fulbert and followed. Lotulpt went out to the three who had been waiting and said, "He gave his consent." Turning to me, he asked threateningly, "Are you with us?"

Without speaking, Lotulpt and his band of strangers proceeded deliberately to their appointed task with me in tow. The pace was quick and relentless. The air seemed to be getting thicker and thicker with each step so that soon, I feared, I would be unable to inhale it because of its increasing viscosity.

At Abelard's door I heard someone order, "Cover your face," and saw the flash of a blade just before they rushed in to surprise the slumbering Abelard. Two of the men pinned him back on his bed, while the other with the knife made his approach. Lotulpt stood off in a corner of the room, while I remained outside. I heard the muffled sounds of their struggle and then a sharp scream of pain.

Everyone rushed from the scene and scattered in all directions. In my delirium, I could only manage to move around to the corner of the building, just barely out of sight. From there I saw Abelard stagger to his doorway, the front of his once white robe now stained crimson, with blood streaming down his legs and pooling at his feet.

"Father, forgive them," he said as he slumped to the floor.

"For they know not what they do!" I said under my breath to finish the thought. Only I knew! I turned to run away, but instead fell upon my knees and vomited. Lotulpt had accomplished what he wanted. Like the eunuchs relegated to the outer courtyard of Solomon's temple by their deformity, barred from the assembly of holy men and entrance to the inner sanctum, so, too, was Abelard now condemned.

Chapter Ten

Exiled

*T*end to her, as should a brother tend to his deceased brother's wife, for I am dead to this world and have no place in it.

John was the first to come to Abelard's aid. A neighbour had hurried to get him after being awakened by all the commotion caused by the dark episode that had just occurred. After cleaning Abelard up the best he could, John summoned others to help. Fearful for Abelard's life or that another attack might be imminent, John and his friends quickly transported him to the royal abbey by carrying him in a blanket. There they sought further aid and sanctuary for him.

St. Denis' abbey was located in the northern part of the city. The king supported the abbey financially, and the abbot and all the monks supported the king faithfully. It was a mutually rewarding relationship. The king could buy God's goodwill and the abbey prospered by providing it.

The abbot was not particularly happy about having been disturbed in the middle of the night by a group of men with an injured comrade until Abelard's identity was revealed. Then, shivers of glee almost overtook him when one of his monks announced the news, "It is Abelard, father, the once favourite son of the university."

The royal abbey and the university were generally at odds. Members of academia looked down upon the abbey because it had "sold out" to the king. The members of the abbey, on the other hand, felt that the university was full of hypocritical moralists who sought vain fame by postulating new theses and vying for the most prestigious positions in the Church. To harbour one of the university's outcasts was a coup for the abbey, and, so, Abelard was treated well, almost as a celebrity, throughout the halls of St. Denis. The abbot once confided to Abelard that, "At first I considered you a prize to flaunt before the snobbish hierarchy of the university." Later, however, the abbot said that he had come to prize Abelard for more esoteric reasons.

The day after the attack on Abelard, Thessaly had sought me out to discover for Héloïse what I knew about her beloved's fate. Thessaly said that Fulbert had indicated to Héloïse that I might know more than I was saying. Thessaly took up my defence and told them both, "Alberic is friend, not foe, to Abelard. He would have had nothing to do with any devious plot against him."

"Thank you, Thessaly," I said, "For shielding my honour."

"Think nothing of it," she replied, "You are a kind man, a thoughtful man, not a villain such as some who operate only for personal gain or glory. But, Héloïse is very worried. The whereabouts of Abelard is not known. Is he dead, dear Alberic? If that is the case, be compassionate and reveal it so that we may go on with our grief. But, if he is not, pray tell us, and where he resides, so that Héloïse may go to him, for I fear for her safety as well."

"No one should harm her now that Abelard is gone," I responded. "With him went the shame."

"There may remain some yet unrevealed shame," she said.

"John knows well where Abelard is recovering. Go ask him."

"Recovering from what?" gasped Thessaly.

"Do not worry," I said to console her, "He is fine. But John knows the details better than I do."

With a big hug around my neck, Thessaly thanked me for the information and went off to see John. I knew she would convince John to tell her Abelard's secret location, so I said, "Tell me how you find Abelard."

"Oh, I will," she replied, "I'll tell you everything."

I really did not know what had happened to Abelard for certain after the incident. Through Thessaly is how I found out most of the story. She always confided the latest gossip about our mutual friends and acquaintances to me. I hoped that too much of the story was never made known to her.

It was not surprising that meddling John did not even hesitate to let Héloïse know where Abelard was lodged. How could he put her in such harm's way? Going to Abelard so presently would display complicity with the whole affair and force Fulbert in a position that might cause her to be disowned or sent away. Nonetheless, without considering all the consequences, John took Héloïse and Thessaly straightaway to the abbey of St. Denis to see Abelard. If I had been in John's place, I would have kept vague the condition and whereabouts of Abelard in order to protect Héloïse from further distress.

When they arrived at the abbey, the three of them were escorted to an anteroom connected to the main sanctuary of the chapel to wait for Abelard. It was not long before Abelard appeared in brilliant white raiment and slowly walked toward them.

"Abelard, my dearest love," Héloïse cried as she rushed to embrace him. Abelard remained rigid and unresponsive. "Abelard, why so cold; where is the warmth of your embrace?"

"Do you know what has happened to me? The horror?" he asked her grimly.

"I know, dear one, what has happened, but can only guess the horror of it all. Yet, the shame is not on you. The shame is upon the villains who performed the deed. Theirs is eternal damnation for what was done to a worthy man."

"I am not the man I was," he told her.

"You are still the man I love," she countered sweetly.

"How can I be?" he said angrily. "The shame I bear is rightly deserved! I was not the man you loved the moment I yielded to your love. Our love marred my soul and now my body has been marred in just proportions."

"How can you speak of our love in such a way?" Héloïse pleaded. "Our love was joy, and our souls reached upward, and we felt that God was surely smiling upon us. Our love was fresh, without evil, a gift from the Creator as surely as life itself."

Abelard grabbed Héloïse's shoulders. "Search your soul and see the terrible toll this love has taken on our piety."

Héloïse retaliated by saying, "Search your heart and see how false piety has kept your soul from loving." Abelard turned and walked a few feet away. "You love me still. I can see it in your eyes."

Abelard turned back to her and pronounced, "Then only in my eyes will you see the love that is stored inside for you.

Yes, my hand trembles to touch you and my arms ache to embrace you, but when I reach out there must be nothing and I shall have silence as my bedfellow."

"Oh, Abelard, my love," she implored, "It is not destined to be so! I will let my feelings out and scream to the world of my love for you. I will be unashamed and straightforward and tell all who will hear that I love you."

"Héloïse!" he chided, "I have given up the man fate destined me to be in order to love you. Now, I have been made even less of a man because of that love. What more must I say?"

"That it was not worth it," she immediately replied.

"What?" he asked, staggered by her reply.

"Tell me that love is not worth any sacrifice. It is worth everything in God's eyes, 'For God so loved the world that he gave his only begotten son.'" Héloïse moved close to Abelard and asked, "Is one's destiny so full it cannot make room for love?"

"I remember a story you once told us, Abelard," began John as he stepped up to the couple onto whom he had been eavesdropping. "This man took a large earthen vase and filled it to the brim with large rocks and asked, 'Is the vase full?' To his question those watching him replied, 'Yes, it is full.' He then took small gravel and poured it into the vase, and there was room for a large quantity of it. 'Now is it full?' he asked. The spectators were less sure, but they still said, 'Yes, it is full now.' He then brought sand, and poured a large amount of it into the vase until it piled up on the top to overflowing. "Now it is most surely full," he said to those watching, and they all agreed. Then he said, 'These rocks, and gravel, and sand are like the trials, the problems, and inconveniences, both large and small that fill your life to the brim.' He then drew water from a nearby well and began pouring it into the vase. He poured, and poured, and the spectators could not believe how much water the vase could hold even though it had already appeared full. 'But the water permeates our life with hope, joy, and love and fills every void.' Do you remember that story, my friend?"

"Yes, John," Abelard answered, "The water symbolizes La Paracléte, the Holy Spirit, and the interconnecting, through the Spirit, of one person to another." The three embraced. "Forgive my self-pity. How I love you both!" Héloïse motioned to Thessaly. "And, Thessaly, come join our reuniting."

Thessaly came close to the group and received an exuberant hug from John. "One thing more," interposed Héloïse. "Thessaly, as dear companion, once delivered me to Paris, and will deliver me again as midwife, for I am with child."

This time Héloïse received one of John's rough hugs. "Careful," warned Thessaly.

"Oh, she is strong of will and body, she can take it," replied John while giving Héloïse a second hard hug.

Abelard appeared shaken as he spoke softly to Héloïse. "My responsibilities to you have multiplied, and I am in no position to assume them. Go to Thessaly's convent at Argenteuil," he instructed her. "The sisterhood can make safe and secure anyone it wishes to protect."

"Yes," added Thessaly, "We can make you vanish from sight."

"You would send me off, exile me, from all I have come to love?" asked Héloïse. "Have I found you only to lose you again?"

Abelard looked at her gently and said, "You have not lost me. You will never lose me again. I will always be with you, if not in the flesh, in spirit."

Thessaly and John moved off to leave the couple alone to say their parting words to one another. Abelard and Héloïse stood as close as they could without actually touching each other. One spoke while the other listened intently. Then the other spoke while the listener kept silent to take in all that was being said. Their exchange went on for some time until Abelard walked Héloïse over to the other two who had been patiently waiting. He then charged his friends with the care of Héloïse by saying, "John, this is my wife and the mother of my child. Tend to her, as should a brother tend to his deceased brother's wife, for I am dead to this world and have no place in it. Thessaly, this is your sister." Then putting Thessaly's hand on Héloïse's abdomen he said, "Héloïse, this is the child's aunt. She will see to its delivery and share in its upbringing." Abelard took a few steps away from the others and then said, "Go now, for the longer you stay, the harder it becomes to let you go. My love to all of you, and especially my love I send with you, Héloïse, my wife; may it sustain and comfort you, like your love does me."

"Write to me," called Héloïse through her tears as she started to leave.

"Write me back," called Abelard. "And tell me how my garden grows, for through that coded message only privileged eyes will know that you share with me the condition of those I cherish most."

So began what John called, "The greatest love affair ever conducted by letters alone," since the two hardly ever saw each other again. I know that was the case because Thessaly and I served as intermediaries for them and delivered many of their messages to one another over the years. However, I never understood how Abelard could let someone he professed to love face childbirth and life alone. He should have been there. Someone should have been there for her.

Instead, for a time, Abelard remained at the abbey in relative comfort and safety. However, for him, monastic walls were too limiting, and his restlessness soon saw him into trouble. As a diversion from the boredom that had set in, he spent a great deal of time in the expansive library of St. Denis and made some startling discoveries about the origin of the abbey. Abelard always possessed a propensity for uncovering information that led to complications and controversy. One day, he discovered an ancient manuscript tucked away in an abandoned storage cubicle that disclosed the long-forgotten, or long-hidden and wantonly ignored, story of this most renowned abbey. Written documents are so precious that no man would have the heart to destroy even the most libellous of works. And, so, the manuscript had merely collected dust for centuries in storage, where it should have remained under cover except that Abelard was never content with the status in quo.

The document revealed a major error concerning the founding of the abbey. The saint, Denis, was also known as Dionysius. According to the account Abelard had recently discovered, Denis set out from Rome around 250 A.D. to teach the gospel to the inhabitants of Gaul. He spent his life among the common folk of the land and ministered without pretence or glory to their physical and spiritual needs. He was servant to the servant and brought dignity to the dispossessed and downtrodden people of the region who were being governed so harshly by the hand of Rome.

Denis and his two companions, a priest and a deacon, settled on an island near the present city of Paris and continued their ministry to the people. The Roman governor of that part of Gaul was annoyed by this Christian influence and indirect interference with his authority, so he ordered the arrest of Denis and his two friends. The text Abelard had uncovered went on to graphically describe how the three men were mercilessly tortured before finally being publicly beheaded. This gruesome tale then added what must be more legend than truth. It stated that Denis arose after his execution and walked several paces through the large crowd of spectators carrying his head in his hand! Hundreds fell upon their knees and converted to Christianity at once. The victory was lost to the Roman governor, and the Faith flourished in the region from that time forth.

How all this relates to the abbey was included in this manuscript that dates to its founding in 626 A.D. The bodies of the three men were thrown into the Seine, but were recovered by a Christian woman named Catulla. She and some of Denis' followers gave them a proper burial and later a chapel was built over their graves. On the same site, Dagobert I, king of the Franks, founded the Abbey of St. Denis over three and a half centuries after its namesake's martyrdom.

Now, Abelard contended this was a worthy founding and lifted it up as the most historically correct, but it was counter to the prevailing predisposition about the abbey's pedigree. After a couple hundred more years of its retelling, the legend of St. Denis was projected back to the earliest days of Christianity. The 9th century leadership of the abbey had falsely identified the martyred Dionysius (Denis) with Dionysius the Aeropagite who was personally converted to Christianity by Saint Paul and who also became the first bishop of Athens. This new version confused and exaggerated the legend of St. Denis and led to the claim that he was sent on his evangelical mission by Pope Clement I, a friend to both Peter and Paul.

Naturally, the close association of the Abbey of St. Denis with the first apostles of Christendom was a source of pride for the abbey's members and especially for the royal family who supported it financially. When Abelard publicly announced that the abbey was indeed founded upon the converter of the barbarians instead of the companion of the apostles, he was summoned to the abbot's chamber.

"How dare you defame this abbey!" shouted the abbot with a face flushed scarlet with rage. "King Louis entrusted us with his son's upbringing. The young heir to the throne must not have his residency so dishonoured."

"Such vain pride in tradition, form, and structure," countered Abelard. "You hide the truth to preserve those things of lesser worth."

"I will not bear any debate on the matter," insisted the abbot. "We treated you with kindness, and you treat us so! You came to us wounded in body and repay us by wounding us spiritually."

"Spirit is not the same as reputation of which you seem most concerned," argued Abelard.

"We give you protection and you disrespect our sanctuary," the abbot stated through clenched teeth. "The king is also furious. He is considering criminal charges against you, Abelard!"

"Criminal charges?" asked the incredulous Abelard. "Is the world on such an insecure foundation that one dissenting voice can make it tremble and quake over such a trivial fault?"

"Yes, I suppose it is," acquiesced the unapologetic abbot. "The king will put you on trial for your libellous comments, and I will not impede your arrest by upholding your right of sanctuary against his indictments."

"Then you turn me over to worldly authority instead of upholding God's authority," accused Abelard.

"No, I do not," said the once again angered abbot. "Why do I disclose the king's intent to you if that was so? I do not know what God has in store for you, but I do know what King Louis will do to you, prison at least, or possibly death because of the contempt you would undoubtedly display to his court. My hope is that your abjuring the realm will demonstrate enough remorse and repentance to placate Louis so that he might not pursue your case but attend to more kingly matters."

Abelard was slightly shaken by the abbot's suggestion. He stepped up to the chamber's large window, "Out there," he said, "Are many other dangers destined to befall me."

The abbot laid an arm across Abelard's shoulders and with a softer voice said, "My son, always remember what Saint Paul wrote in his second epistle to the Corinthians, beginning with the third verse, 'Blessed be the God and Father of our Lord Jesus Christ, the Father of mercies and God of all comfort, who comforts us in all our affliction, so that we may be able to comfort those who are in any affliction.' It is our commission to comfort others not ourselves. If we face life with Paul's point of view, then whatever happens to us is inconsequential. La Paraclète is our comfort and consoler. You must go before the guard arrives. You have only a short time."

Abelard turned to go, but hesitated, and without turning back to meet the abbot's eyes, he said, "I will never forget you, your counsel, and your kindness."

The abbot also turned his back on Abelard before saying, "I will miss you, too, my son."

With nowhere to go, this was just the beginning of a succession of, what must have been for him, bitter disappointments and trying times. Of course, he could not return to the university and face Fulbert's wrath. The royal abbey would never again grant him sanctuary. The king's guards were looking for him. Héloïse was lost to him. He had become a fugitive from all that must have been important to him. No longer was he the proud and resilient person he used to be. He was a beaten man. Even his friends did not give him aid.

To add more insult to injury, a cabal of Abelard's powerful enemies insisted that Church authorities review his theological work, *On the Divine Unity and Trinity*, during an ecclesiastical council meeting at Soissons. With no one in attendance to defend the work, it was quickly condemned and burned as a warning of how such heresy would be dealt with in the future.

Abelard wandered aimlessly, seeking asylum outside the purview of Parisian officials. He travelled northeast into the territory controlled by Count Theobald of Champagne and was well received by the count. Kindness was lavished upon him by this household to such an extent that the only way Abelard could repay it was to leave so that no harm would come to the count or his family for harbouring him. Theobald professed that he did not feel threatened by Church or Crown in the matter, yet Abelard insisted that it would be better for him to move on.

Again wandering in the wilderness, Abelard happened across an abandoned hermit's hut near Norgent-sur-Seine. It had been vacant for years, but was a suitable residence for a man with his mental condition. This crude and primitive structure, with leaky roof and draughty walls, barely stood at all. The walls were so short that a person of average height would have to stoop when inside. They were constructed of wood slats and the gaps between the irregular boards were plastered with mud. Over time, rain had washed much of the mud away, leaving big holes in the sides of the building. The thatch roof had been repeatedly patched with muddy sod until the weight of the repairs caused some parts of it to cave in. The whole structure leaned precariously, and only a mound of dirt piled against the most acutely angled wall prevented its total collapse. Its inhabitant was also close to total collapse.

Abelard no longer took heed to personal grooming. He had become filthy by living in such squalor. He no longer washed himself or his garments. His hair grew long and his beard grew shaggy. He ate little and became emaciated.

In his desolation he seemed to forget how to speak and only mumbled incoherently to himself. He maintained a daily routine of mere subsistence, picking up small twigs and branches for a fire, gathering berries and nuts from the forest, and travelling to a shallow stream to fill a small container with water. He only acquired enough of those items each day to last the day.

The months wore on and I went to visit Héloïse at Argenteuil when I thought it was close to her time. She, too, had been driven from all she held dear. Héloïse had been forced to this place by Abelard's hand, and her condition was as deplorable as his. She no longer basked in the warmth of public acceptance and respect as the brilliant niece of the renowned Fulbert. As an outcast she was hidden away to avoid further shame upon herself. The loss of the fame they both had once achieved must have been the bitterest loss of all for them, even above the loss of each other.

Upon my arrival, I was escorted to the bedchamber where Héloïse was being attended to by Thessaly and some other nuns. Héloïse's face was dripping with sweat and at times she emitted deep groans of distress.

"Alberic," said Héloïse between moments of discomfort, "I am so glad to see you!"

"Oh, Héloïse," I responded, "I am so sorry to see you in such a state!"

Héloïse almost laughed, "This is not my deathbed, you know. Instead, it is a place to bring forth life, so be joyful for me."

I did not know how to respond. Then, to my great surprise, in charged John with pails of hot water and fresh linen. "I do not know of what use these are, but is there anything else you ladies need?" he asked of the nuns.

Thessaly got up from the side of the bed where she had been clutching Héloïse's hand, grabbed my hand instead, and gently said, "Now, you two should step outside and leave us to our business."

"Yes, indeed," agreed John as he started for the door.

"Wait," called Héloïse. "Dear sisters, could I have a word alone with these gentlemen?" Thessaly began to protest. "I will be fine," insisted Héloïse, "Only a moment."

Thessaly obediently led the other nuns from the room to leave John and me alone with Héloïse. "Come close, please," said Héloïse. We moved next to her bed, I on one side and John on the other. She held our hands. Before speaking again, she paused to look at us intensely, first at me and then at John. "This is not the place to raise a child," she explained, "When it is time, you must take the child and raise it properly." Then looking back at me she continued, "It must be taught wisely and kept safe from evil."

"A child needs a mother," said John.

"And a father," I added.

"And so it shall always have," replied Héloïse as her grip on John's hand tightened enough that I could see her knuckles turning white, "But, promise you will see to its care. For a while, be mother and father. Promise me."

"Of course!" responded John strong enough for both of us.

Héloïse let out a more pronounced cry that quickly brought Thessaly and the nuns back into the room. "Now, shoo!" Thessaly scolded us, "Go, and wait outside."

John and I stayed just on the other side of Héloïse's door and carried on a light conversation to pass the time, but my mind wandered amid other thoughts. Since I had learned where Abelard had taken refuge at the moment, it was surprising that others such as John did not seem to know, or did not appear to care. Or, perhaps they did not want to tell Héloïse about her husband's whereabouts as pretence to excuse him for his absence at this important event. And, what of Héloïse's charge to John and me? How were we supposed to care for the child of Abelard? Was it destined to face the same abandonment from Abelard as its mother, to be exiled to a distant place far from those who should love him?

The attitude of John was perplexing. He seemed cheerful and excited. Had he not considered all these things? There was much being asked of him and of me. The responsibility of rearing a child was great and inopportune for both of us. We had lives full of aspirations, just as Abelard once did, and they should not be disrupted by the self-centredness of others.

Due to my musing on these matters, I did not notice that the chamber's doorway behind me had opened until John rushed over to Thessaly who was waiting therein. Into his outstretched arms she delivered what appeared to be no more than a squirming bundle of cloth. Gently digging down toward the centre of the bundle, John revealed something that caused a big smile to come upon his face. Thessaly smiled at John's elation and then looked at me. She offered me a smile, but I was in no mood to return it.

"Little one," cooed John, "Your loving father has chosen a name with special meaning for your christening," but he would not divulge it. "It is a surprise for the mother," he said with a wink to Thessaly and a smile through the doorway to Héloïse.

"This child shall prove the measure of Abelard and Héloïse's lofty worth."

I could not share in everyone's exuberance, for my mind laboured with thoughts about yet another life destined for rejection and loneliness.

Chapter Eleven

Resurrection

*Y*ou know all these things, so why not abide by them and live life anew?

John stepped toward the frail and sullen man and recited scripture from the book of Matthew, "The very stone which the builders rejected will become the head of the corner. That is your destiny," he added, "It has not been altered. You shall inspire great schools of thought while those who have persecuted you will be erased from memory."

John, along with his protégés, Peter Lombard Berenger and Arnold of Brescia, had once again crowded into Abelard's domicile, a different location, perhaps, but for the same purpose. "You are not guilty of any offence," noted Peter, "It is the others who should bear the guilt, yet you suffer for it."

Abelard's mud hut could hardly house the three visitors who had come to rescue its inhabitant from its gloomy interior. "You shall be vindicated!" exclaimed Arnold who had become impassioned by the sight of the pitifully weakened man he held in such high regard.

Abelard had backed into a shadowy corner. He must have become even more frail and ragged than when I saw him last.

His eyes were sunken into their sockets and unresponsive. The visitors later described him as "a walking corpse." John moved over to him and gently grabbed his hand. "Master," he said, "You have led us all to the light. Now allow us to do so for you."

With shuffling steps, Abelard followed John's lead to the door. Upon its opening, Abelard was blinded by the bright sunlight, but he continued out with the assistance, and by the insistence, of John. With eyes closed, Abelard was startled by a loud noise all around him. He squinted to see an army of men cheering his emergence from the earthen tomb. Tears began to stream down from his then wide-opened eyes.

Peter and Arnold had recruited many of their friends to join them in finding Abelard and following his teachings. They were all as pent-up soldiers ready to fight for some righteous cause. Abelard's distancing himself from the established Church served to make him popular with the young and questioning students of the day. His persecution, in their minds, gave him heroic proportions. They were ready to march wherever their general would lead.

I believe that John had incited these naïve young men into thinking this way. He had guided them to this place, not just physically, but mentally and emotionally. If this situation went sour, the blame would be on him.

These new disciples of Abelard saw to his daily needs. They set up tents and gathered food. Abelard's health improved and he again became robust in both mind and body. The mud hut was straightened and repaired, not dismantled as one might expect, and became the camp's centrepiece. It served as Abelard's sanctuary, well lit with candles and furnished with an easel for writing.

Abelard's fame spread throughout the countryside and beyond into all of Christendom. Students, scholastics, teachers and mentors, the sick in spirit and the strong of faith, came to hear his word. Yes, the crowds came, and often I was among them, and I marvelled at Abelard's effect over such congregations that were not really being exposed to any new revelations from his teaching.

When Abelard saw the crowds, he would go to the top of a small hill near his hut and sit down. John and Peter would usually join him and sit beside him – John on his right with Peter on his left. Sometimes, if Abelard knew of my presence before he had made his move up the mound, he would ask me to join them. It was exhilarating to look down upon the sea of people who had gathered and feel the rising tide of energy as they waited for the moment of Abelard's first utterance.

"Never forget that you are blessed when men revile you and persecute you and say all kinds of evil against you falsely for righteousness' sake. Whoever understands and follows and teaches men so, shall be called great in the Kingdom of God; 'For I tell you, unless your righteousness exceeds that of the scribes and Pharisees, you will never enter the kingdom of heaven.'"

Abelard masterfully used scriptures to make personal points, to denounce criticism of him, and to attack the Church establishment of which he was becoming an ever more threatening enemy.

At the end of his sermon, no matter what the topic, Abelard would rise to make his final statement and farewell. Lifting up his hand to the crowd he would say something such as, "You know all these things, so why not abide by them and live life anew? A resurrection is in store for all of you, in this life and into the next, if you but live by what you know is true."

Whenever he was finished with what he was saying, the crowds seemed astounded by his teachings. I often felt that his comments expressed simplistic ideas and wondered why they evoked such emotion. The doctrine of the Church was not dissimilar to Abelard's words, except that the Church tries harder to help people understand what is "true" rather than leaving them to wander aimlessly in their own search to find it out.

Abelard's encampment of followers lasted almost a year, from spring to spring. The winter in between had been unusually mild and caused no particular hardship on the ever-growing number of people who came to spend time listening to Abelard. When people came they brought an abundance of food with them and shared it with those who resided with Abelard on a more permanent basis. If a large crowd gathered, it was similar to the Biblical feeding of the five thousand. Seemingly, there would never be enough food to feed the hungry throng, yet after everyone had been fed and satisfied, there was yet a surplus.

During this period of time, Abelard wrote his *Scito te ipsum* or "Know Thyself" treatise. In this work he re-analyzed his previous position on sin and confirmed his earlier, and still drastic, conclusion that human actions do not make a man better or worse in the sight of God, for he claimed that deeds themselves are neither bad nor good. He continued to emphasize that what is important to God are a man's intentions; sin is not something done, it is uniquely the consent of the human mind to what it knows is wrong. I mention his position again because this analysis by Abelard seemed awfully convenient to many in the established Church. It sounded as a way for Abelard to rationalize his own actions, to repress his guilt, and to forgo his need for personal repentance. This brought increasing resentment toward him from those who knew well what he had done, but those who now lived in close proximity to his sacred mud hut accepted his philosophy at face value.

Meanwhile, life had not stood still for others. Héloïse had become prioress, or second in charge, at the convent at Argenteuil. Even though Héloïse possessed an irrepressible personality and high intellect, this meteoric rise was remarkable and probably occurred through a higher authority's intervention. According to John, this was not a joyous change in status for Héloïse because it meant a change in her relationship with Abelard. Her marriage to him would have had to been made null, for her marriage was now to God. John said that, through letters, Abelard counselled the unwilling Héloïse to take the veil at Argenteuil. Once again he denied her.

The nuns at Argenteuil quickly began to revere Héloïse. She educated her sisters in subjects usually solely reserved to men of the cloth, lifted the nun's status in the Church's hierarchy to one equal that of men, and made everyone feel that their part in doing God's work on earth was important no matter how menial it may appear to be. Her work was becoming recognized and appreciated by the less 'enfranchised' members of the Church. I admired her vision and tenacity in working toward the accomplishment of her goals.

All the while in Paris, Fulbert and I maintained a casual relationship. I stopped visiting him as regularly because we seemed to have run out of topics of conversation unless it centred around the dilemma of doing what is considered right as opposed to heeding the leading of one's heart, to which I always replied, "It is not the matter of either; it is obedience to God that should determine our actions."

"Is that so?" he would often irritatingly respond.

Even after a year, the fate of Abelard and Héloïse still weighed heavily on his mind. Another reason that I saw less of him was because Fulbert had convinced the abbot of St. Denis that I would be a capable historian for his library. I gladly accepted the position and later became the head of the entire library. My propensity for philology and my accurate evaluating and recording of historic events became so respected by the Church and Crown that I was supplied with a large staff and given the task of transcribing and translating volumes of ancient manuscripts. Lotulpt and I sometimes accompanied Bernard to Rome where I was afforded the luxury of studying at the extensive papal library.

So, the next couple of years went relatively smoothly for us all. Everyone kept busy and let the recent past unhappy events fade from memory. Near his Norgent-sur-Seine encampment, Abelard directed his efforts toward the construction of a permanent facility. Funded by wealthy sponsors who were enraptured by Abelard's new religious movement, the construction went quickly. Craftsmen from all around the neighbouring countryside took turns working on the project. Some volunteered their time while others were hired as supervisors over the unskilled labourers who consisted mainly of Abelard's students.

First to be constructed was a modest church. Well-built and architecturally pleasing, Abelard would not permit its interior to be ornately decorated. He wanted no statuary or iconic impressions. The blank walls, he believed, would induce the mind to wonder freely about the nature of God. He did not want the artist's brush or sculptor's chisel to create preconceived notions about things intangible. Even though he claimed to appreciate their talents, he preferred the musician's talent more because its manifestation was also intangible and allowed the mind its own interpretations. Somehow music was supposed to help us know the unknowable, but I never understood how that fit in with his precept of understanding things through reason. Music is not reasonable. It is perceived. This again is an example of the many dichotomies I have discovered with Abelard and his thinking.

The student workers had continued living in tents and cooked their meals over open fires during the construction of the church. It was now time to provide them with better amenities. At a right angle to the back of the church was built the refectory, or dining hall. It housed large stone ovens, a storeroom full of provisions, and enough wooden tables and benches to seat a hundred people. Across from the refectory, also at a right angle with the church, was built the dormitory. Finally, to complete the square, a guesthouse and a residence for Abelard was built directly opposite the church. The buildings enclosed a large courtyard that was surrounded by a sheltering arcade along its perimeter called the cloister. Within this cloistered area, Abelard and his followers would be able to enjoy peaceful reflection and discussion.

However, Abelard never occupied the residence, never walked the finished courtyard, and never even dedicated the church. Upon the project's completion, though, he named the place La Paraclète and then made a startling announcement. He was going to make arrangements for Héloïse to become abbess of this new convent that he had just caused to be built. John said that he did all of this without ever seeing Héloïse in the process, but I doubt that possible. He asserted that, through correspondence only, Abelard set forth rules and composed songs of worship for the new order.

Under Héloïse's leadership, and with the continued support of Abelard's patrons, the nunnery flourished. Its service to the people of the area became legendary for its generous dispensation of real and spiritual food. Héloïse knew that she could not feed a hungry spirit if the person had a hungry stomach. Affluence and comfort were not commonplace in the territories outside of such places as Paris, so there was much work for her nuns to do. At Héloïse's request, Abelard arranged for the acquisition of more land around the convent and had it cleared and made tillable. The nuns planted huge gardens of vegetables and sowed fields of wheat and barley. Through skill, diligent effort, and the blessings of a benevolent God, their harvest was always bountiful enough to share with the less fortunate.

Abelard had conducted the accomplishment of all these things as a vagabond. He had no place of his own to lay his head. He seemed content with his existence and made no complaints about its inconvenience. The original encampment of his followers around the mud hut had moved to the edge of La Paracléte during its construction, but it was now time for it to be moved again since the work there was done. Everyone was anticipating Abelard's next move, and, yet, when it became revealed, it was totally unexpected.

Chapter Twelve

Battle Lines

*S*o, *the battle lines were drawn between the powerful and the pathetic, but I swore no sympathies for either side.*

Abelard mobilized his troops. He, along with his right-hand man, John, and a number of his followers marched on Paris and set up camp on the lower south bank of the Seine. This move surprised many, including myself, who thought he would never dare return to the city he had so offended. Abelard's band lingered there for many weeks as if waiting for Paris to make the first move. Abelard's inactivity kept those huddled inside the great halls of the university and royal abbey wondering and anxious. Aggravatingly to them, he was doing nothing. He did not lecture publicly. He remained inconspicuous in all ways, but his presence, nonetheless, was being felt.

Abelard's ranks began to swell steadily, not only with new recruits from the outlying areas of Paris, but also with deserters from within the inner sanctum of the city. Abelard soon had to give up his unassuming ways to appease the rapid influx of new followers. He began holding scheduled lectures and started writing proficiently in what John described as a "blaze of glory." University students would take off from their regular studies to hear Abelard speak and even some scholastics and monks attended his lectures. This was all becoming too much for the university and for the abbot of St. Denis to ignore, so old enemies became new allies. A meeting was called between the university and the royal abbey. By invitation of the abbot, I was in attendance.

One of the university's canons selected to participate in the meeting spoke first, "There is a menace at our doorstep with which we must deal. We are all familiar with his propaganda and its allure with the younger, less astute, students of the university."

"Yes, that is *your* problem," replied the outwardly complacent abbot, "How does this possibly involve me or my abbey?"

"With all due respect, Dear Abbot," began another representative of the university, "We need to consider that he often lectures in our native tongue instead of Latin, and sometimes conducts religious services among his followers."

Again the abbot responded indifferently, "I do not really think that is much of a threat to us. If Abelard is leading people to the Faith, then the complaints you present about his methods are somewhat trivial."

"Trivial?" snapped one of the canons, "How is it that the discovery of the true namesake of your abbey is issue enough to evict him from your sanctuary, but the stealing of our students is such a trivial offence?"

Just then, in walked Lotulpt. "I apologize for my tardiness," he said.

"What news have you brought us?" asked one of the canons.

"Bernard is unable to attend this meeting," explained Lotulpt. "But I assure you he will support you in this matter."

"We have come to no decisions on the matter," concluded the abbot.

"Then maybe you should know this," suggested Lotulpt. "There is more to Abelard's teachings than just his continuous heresy. He is attempting to dismantle the Church and its fundamental principles by encouraging revolt against our ways."

"How so?" asked the abbot raising an eyebrow in doubt.

"By professing that the Church has no business being involved with the politics and government of the state," replied Lotulpt.

"Render under Caesar's that which is Caesar's, but unto God what is God's," I interjected.

"What does Bernard suggest we do?" asked the abbot.

"Dear Abbot and honourable canons," began Lotulpt, "This affair is distasteful and dirty. Bernard felt that such work might be beneath your positions as respected leaders of the Church. You should wash your hands of it. We have found a willing adversary against Abelard. You can remain above the fray and appear neutral in the conflict. Proceeding in such a fashion, your students will not feel that the university is responsible, nor will the people find fault with your abbey for being the cause of Abelard's ultimate demise."

"And who is this champion to fight our cause?" asked one of the canons.

"William of Saint-Thierry and the abbey of Saint Victor," answered Lotulpt smugly.

I understood what this all meant. At one time William had been an admirer of Abelard, but more recently he had been swayed to an opposite persuasion. William and Bernard, along with the members of the abbey of Saint Victor, held similar beliefs regarding mysticism that were in marked contrast to Abelard's humanistic approach to Christianity. Bernard often colourfully described the mystic experience by saying, "Knowledge of God is similar to a great flash of light," a reference, no doubt, to the conversion of Saint Paul, "And the eye-opening revelation of God's truth is blinding by its brilliance."

William and Bernard both believed that intuitive knowledge of God could be attained through deep, personal religious experiences, but William felt that the type of these experiences was not as important as the quality of life that follows them. In the early days of Abelard's education and subsequent teaching, because he demonstrated the qualities of vitality, productivity, joy, inner peace, and harmony with God that are the natural issuances of a mystical life, William found no great incompatibility with his own beliefs and Abelard's quest for knowledge. Bernard's supporters, who did not want their man to have his hands sullied by dealing with the problem, had somehow managed to change William's views and set him up as the unwitting scapegoat for anything that might go wrong during the ensuing attacks on Abelard.

The abbey of Saint Victor was located some forty miles northeast of Paris and its members had been studiously critical of Abelard's doctrines. The monks had collected Abelard's works and researched accepted historical authorities that would refute his theological assertions. The abbey became the repository for the ecclesiastical armament needed to finally defeat Abelard if and when a strong enough leader was inclined to launch such an offensive. So, the battle lines were drawn between the powerful and the pathetic, but I swore no sympathies for either side.

Abelard made the first move. He began lecturing at Mont-Sainte Geneviève just outside Paris where it was rumoured he was intending to establish a permanent school. This was particularly insulting to the Parisian religious hierarchy since Geneviève was the patron saint of Paris. In 451 she was in Paris and predicted the invasion of Attila and the Huns, and through her intercessory prayers the city was saved. She then converted Clovis I, king of the Francs, to Christianity and, through him, converted the entire nation. It was blasphemous in the eyes of many church leaders that Abelard would use this place to attempt converting France to his personal precepts.

William was basically powerless, but under great pressure to act. He personally recruited Bernard for direct assistance. Despite his friends' and advisors' recommendations, Bernard decided to intervene. Bernard's supporters had set their sights much higher than at a confrontation with a renegade scholastic. To them, his place was at the Holy City, as counsel to the Holy Father, and maybe as his successor. Then they would reap the rewards of their unwavering support.

Bernard acquiesced to William's plea for assistance by stating that the matter would be handled permanently during the upcoming Council of religious leaders at the city of Sens. The city was located far enough southeast of Paris that not all of Abelard's followers would make the trip, but it would be convenient for Bernard and his supporters who had planned to be in attendance in any case.

The only job left to William was to see that Abelard was also in attendance. William apprehensively prepared to set off to speak to Abelard. He did not know under whose authority he could command Abelard's compliance to Bernard's order for him to attend the Council meeting. It was not a royal decree. It was not an order from Rome. Abelard could resist and William would have no recourse but to withdraw. He asked me to advise him of Abelard's whereabouts and to go with him. He did so not as a courtesy, but because he knew I could obtain cooperation from the royal abbey's guard in the matter. When I told him the time was right, he and I, and four armed soldiers, made out for Abelard's location.

I knew that Abelard often took walks in the woods to escape the crowds that so customarily gathered around him. My contacts with some of Abelard's followers had remained intact despite my association with the royal abbey. They informed me that Abelard was going to spend a couple of days with only his closest friends in a woodland area controlled by Count Theobald. That would be the best possible place to confront Abelard without arousing the ire of a larger population of his followers.

When darkness began to overtake the day, our party made haste to Abelard's camp. Through the trees we could see the orange flickering light of his campfire as we approached. Although our group tried to maintain stealth, Abelard stood to meet us before we had even entered the clearing. John and those who had accompanied Abelard to this place were greatly disturbed by our unexpected arrival. The startled men jumped to their feet while John brandished a small sword in our direction. Abelard raised a hand to stop John and to calm the others. Nonchalantly, I went over to Abelard and greeted him with a hardy embrace.

"Would you betray me with a kiss?" he whispered, and he left his bewildered and silent friends behind to accompany us peacefully to a destiny of which he had no knowledge or seemed to care.

Chapter Thirteen

The Lions' Den

*H*e *had been thrust into the lions' den and was about to be consumed.*

The religious community of France converged on the picturesque city of Sens to hold its periodically called convention. This ancient Gallic city, seated on the Yonne River, was the site of the recently constructed cathedral of Saint-Étienne, an impressive building whose architecture was unlike any other in the whole of France. Its master builders had constructed an elegant building with taller spires and loftier vaults than those erected in previously built churches. To do so, on the outside, they had to lean half arches, with their own massive bases, against the vaults to keep them from spreading outward. The building's façade was covered with delicate stone traceries and its focal point was a rose window of stained glass encased above the cathedral's main entrance. Not only was I impressed by this structure, but also must have been many others. Soon after this visit, the royal abbey of St. Denis began its own construction of a grandiose cathedral of similar design but of significantly larger proportions and with two flanking towers instead of one. Other important religious centres soon became drawn into the competition to outdo other cathedrals in size and majesty in order to demonstrate their higher devotion to God.

On the morning of the Council's convening, I was processing into the cathedral of Saint-Étienne with my fellow scholars and clergy, when someone grabbed the sleeve of my robe to pull me aside.

"Héloïse, Thessaly, what are you doing here," I gasped with astonishment at their unanticipated appearance.

"How could I stay away?" responded Héloïse. "What will take place in the cathedral?"

"A panel of judges will review Abelard's case and determine if he or his works are deserving of condemnation," I explained as succinctly as possible.

"Condemnation for what?" she questioned, "Being truthful and faithful to God?" Then with too loud a voice she declared, "Who are these men who have the right to hold judgment against him?"

"Do not draw attention," I warned her. "Bernard will serve as moderator of course. Lotulpt said that the selection of the other members would demonstrate appropriate impartiality. He said there would be a member from the university, from St. Denis, and that he would also serve on the panel to represent the interests of the larger Church."

"And I have been selected," came a voice from behind our private cluster. We turned and into our midst stepped a tall man of regal bearing. This imposing figure appeared more as a valiant knight than a member of the clergy. His face was well tanned from exposure to the sunlight, not pale as that of those of us whose heads are buried in manuscripts or bowed in prayer for most of the day. His sleek, brown hair fell in waves onto his shoulders and his face was bearded. His eyes were blue, which matched the blue of the regal-looking garment that handsomely covered his obviously rock-hard frame. There was something in the way he spoke and moved that exhibited within him an uncommon dose of inner confidence and relentless optimism. He politely addressed Héloïse. "I could not help but overhear your comment, dear lady, concerning those selected to judge Abelard. How does this matter concern you?"

"I am Héloïse, friend of Abelard, and I seek only fairness in his trial."

"Ah, Héloïse, I have heard of you and your work at Argenteuil," he replied with warmth in his voice. "I have also heard of this Abelard and of his works as well. On my honour, I assure you he will be judged fairly by me."

"And whom do I have the pleasure of meeting?" cordially asked Héloïse who seemed to be enchanted by this person.

"Peter of Cluny," replied the man simply.

"Peter of Cluny," I thought to myself. This was not just simply Peter of Cluny, but the man known better as Peter the Venerable, abbot of Cluny, the elected general of his order, initiator of widespread reform, whose influence was felt by ecclesiastical circles throughout Europe. Who, though he held Bernard in high regard, was more often than not at odds with him. What was Bernard's purpose in selecting him? Did he do it to lend legitimacy to this tribunal, or to disgrace him along with Abelard? Nevertheless, in my estimation, he would undoubtedly somehow end up being Bernard's pawn.

"And you are Alberic from St. Denis," he said as he shook my hand with a strong grip. "You are a member of the panel as well."

I was stunned that he even knew of me. "Yes," I responded rather sheepishly, "I have been selected to serve as the abbey's representative." I was sorry I had not confessed my standing in the matter to Héloïse earlier, but an appropriate moment to do so had not presented itself.

Just then another man came over to speak with Peter to temporarily draw his attention away from us.

"Then you can save Abelard," Thessaly pleaded as she and Héloïse closed in tighter upon me.

"I fear that will be impossible," I replied to the women pressing for my indulgence.

"Why?" Thessaly wondered aloud while backing away from me.

"The vote will be by secret ballot and polled by Bernard. Only he will see the ballots, so, no matter what the vote, the verdict is certain."

"But Bernard is an honourable man!" Thessaly exclaimed.

"Yet a man with too much to lose," I remarked. In order to try to dispel her natural naïveté, I continued to explain. "Bernard is on trial as much as Abelard is; how he handles this situation will be critically viewed by those in attendance who can enable his advancement. He is under enormous pressure to produce the expected outcome from these proceedings."

Peter returned to our discussion.

"I want to go in," announced Héloïse.

"No, that would not be wise," I cautioned. "Your presence could be a distraction to the whole proceeding and may even jeopardize Abelard's case by calling to mind the past and exacerbating old wounds."

"Nonsense," declared Peter as he led the way and escorted the two women into the great hall of the cathedral.

Clergy, scholastics, and prominent laypersons had gathered inside for the typical ecclesiastical discussions conducted at these councils. However, it was a larger crowd than usual because many came to witness the official examination of Abelard's theology. Peter and I continued side-by-side to the front of the church while the two women dropped back. We were met by a mace-bearing cleric who directed us to one of three long wooden tables that were each flanked with two ornately carved chairs. Two of the tables were put parallel across from each other about twenty feet apart. The third table was positioned so that those sitting at it would directly face the audience. In the open area between the tables, a short wooden bench had been set in place. The cleric first escorted Peter to the table where Lotulpt had been seated previously. He then took me to the opposite table where there were still two open chairs. After sitting down, I looked around and saw many strange as well as many familiar faces such as Héloïse and Thessaly, and another familiar one whom I was certainly not expecting to see at this gathering. Last into the cathedral, sitting on a chair that was suspended between two strong poles and carried by four strong monks, was Fulbert.

Since my move from the university to St. Denis, I had not seen the canon often and not for some time, and I was shocked by his current appearance. Fulbert's health had deteriorated greatly and he seemed to be using all his strength just to keep his head upright during the ensuing ride to the front of the sanctuary. I did not know when he had become no longer ambulatory and wondered who was seeing to his care. The monks brought Fulbert to my table and moved him from his portable chair to the one next to mine. He flinched with pain when they tried to put his feet on the floor, so his bearers gently lifted him into place.

"Good morning, Fulbert," I said to him after he had settled into his chair.

"And who might you be?" he asked.

"Alberic, master, it is I, Alberic."

He reached out for my hand and weakly spoke, "Alberic, forgive me, my sight has left me and I did not know your voice."

I was saddened even more by my teacher's frailty and gave him my hand. He set both our hands on the table and patted mine repeatedly. "How good it is that you are here today," he commented.

Looking under the table, I saw the source of much of Fulbert's pain. He wore not sandals or boots of any kind. His feet were loosely wrapped with cloth. Between the rounds of material I could see black and putrefied tissue that extended well above his ankles. I had never seen, but I had been told about such mortification due to injuries sustained in battle. Why Fulbert was subjected to this condition, I did not know. An unpleasant odour from those disgusting appendages began emanating from beneath the table. To my horror I noticed a blackening of the skin on the tips of the fingers of the hand that was holding mine, and I quickly extricated myself from its grip.

Fulbert had become repulsive. I wished that I had never seen him this way. Memories of him when he was strong and vigorous would have been preferable to this vision of him that will be forever engrained in my mind.

The cleric with the mace, an ancient symbol of authority, escorted Abelard from an anteroom to the bench in the middle of the tables, but he would not sit. Abelard kept his back to the assembly of onlookers. I thought to myself, "He had been thrust into the lions' den and was about to be consumed." When he saw Fulbert and me, Abelard came over to our table, smiled at me, and placed his hand on the side of Fulbert's face. "You have never looked better, old man," he said, "At least to me," he added, and he leaned far over the table to kiss the ailing sage on his forehead.

"Abelard, my son," uttered Fulbert with a smile so big it allowed drool to stream from the corner of his mouth.

Such overt politics, I thought. I doubt if Abelard had ever seen Fulbert since he fled Paris. Why now would he try to curry favour from the old man unless it was for personal gain?

Bernard entered from the back of the cathedral and proceeded all the way down its centre aisle. As he made his way, silence began to overcome the congregation. Friendly as well as profound conversations ceased throughout the room as all eyes became trained on Bernard's ascent to his position of authority at the head table. He brushed by Abelard on route to his chair and made not a gesture or spoke not a word to him. He sat. A scribe carrying a load of paper and pen came from a side entrance and positioned himself in the chair next to Bernard to record the event.

Héloïse and Thessaly tried to remain hidden among the crowd, but, surely, Abelard knew they were present. Bernard's informants would have undoubtedly made him aware that they were in the cathedral, yet he tolerated their uninvited presence. Fulbert's poor eyesight would have prevented him from knowing if the two intruders were standing directly in front of him, let alone in the same room with him, unless someone told him, and I certainly was not going to be the one to upset Fulbert by telling him that his estranged niece was close at hand.

Among the others assembled to witness Abelard's interrogation were dignitaries from Rome, members of the Curia, who occupied the front row and who, too, had chairs upon which to sit. The rest of those in attendance would have to stand throughout the entire event just like the congregations of poor churchgoers do at every Mass.

Bernard opened the Council with a cordial greeting to all and a special recognition of the distinguished guests occupying the front row. A lengthy prayer by the local abbot followed. He invoked the understanding and mercy of God to be present in this place. Bernard then introduced the four of us who would sit in judgment over Abelard and briefly explained the procedure for questioning him. With a nod to the Holy City's liaison, he also announced that this panel, "Exists solely to make recommendations to Rome. It is not within this council's purview to condemn a man. The extent of our review is to determine, as educated scholars and representatives of the Church, if the writings and teachings of Abelard warrant condemnation as heresy." He then turned his attention to Abelard. "Pierre Abelard," he said, "Do you have anything to say on your behalf before we begin?"

"How can you separate the work from the man?" asked Abelard. "The two are inseparable. What I write is in me, and what is in me I write. To condemn a man's work is to condemn him personally. No matter how a man appears on the surface, how he acts or what he says publicly, it is what he permanently expresses by the written word that betrays his actual identity."

Bernard quickly replied, "Be it so!" and then he addressed the scribe. "Let it be noted that as far as Abelard is concerned, by his own volition, the condemnation of his works should be regarded as a condemnation of him personally, and the consequences of such condemnation rests squarely upon him as well."

We understood the ramifications of Bernard's statement of record. If even one of Abelard's works, not the entire body of his work, was deserving of condemnation, Bernard could now call for the complete condemnation and censure of Abelard the person. On the surface, this may seem to be inconsequential, but it could make an excommunicatory difference to Abelard.

You already know well the crux of the disagreements between Bernard and Abelard. As Abelard's works were reviewed, Bernard often became loud and animated in his argument. Lotulpt was constantly trying to proselytize the audience to Bernard's position with both lofty phrases and subtle innuendos. Peter and I remained relatively silent, and I am not sure whether Fulbert even knew what went on most of the time. Surprisingly though, throughout it all, Abelard remained calm and collected. His arguments were pointed and logical, however that did not necessarily help his cause since logic often seemed on trial as well.

Throughout the day, Bernard prosecuted Abelard's case with verve, and Lotulpt prosecuted it too vigorously. Lotulpt kept dapping at the surface of issues with remarks he hoped would cause Abelard to take the bait and lure him on the hook. However, Abelard remained resolute and appeared to be winning many arguments and winning the hearts and minds of many as well. Out of frustration, Lotulpt retreated from his frontal attack and resorted to another, more devious, approach. Lotulpt rose from his chair. "Tell me, Abelard," he began while looking out into the crowd, "With all your pious rhetoric, how is it that your life denies what you preach? How can you stand here as a man of God with treachery and deceit in your heart, knowing well you mock your vows of celibacy and obedience, and not confess that your words and actions defy the very things the Church most aspires to be?"

"How can you stand here as well then?" asked Abelard bluntly.

Lotulpt reeled around to confront Abelard. "You dare make such innuendo about me! You have no evidence to support your accusations, but I do mine, half man!" There was a low rumble from the entire assembly.

Peter was compelled to interrupt. "This is argumentum ad hominem!" he protested. "It is beneath our discussions! Keep to the proper matters at hand, Lotulpt, for you will sway no one with your gossip."

"They are facts, and it is Abelard who said that we cannot separate the works from the man!" countered Lotulpt angrily.

"Stop!" shouted Bernard as he rose with arms uplifted. "I will have a conference with the judges – except for you Fulbert. Stay and rest. We will return in just a moment." Bernard led Peter, Lotulpt and me to a private anteroom before continuing his dialogue, but Peter had the first words.

"I know what you would have this panel do," said Peter firmly to Bernard. "But, if I condemn Abelard and his works, I condemn myself and you as well, for we have asked similar questions about our faith if not publicly, at least privately. There is no heresy in honest questioning. There is no blasphemy in believing in God no matter what form was used to develop that belief. Abelard is a man of God. He is not intending to tear down the Church, but to build it up to greater glory by exposing and breaking its worldly bonds. I will not be your puppet in this case. I will vote my conscience."

"You think your loyalty to the Church is so beyond reproach that you can make such bold statements?" threatened Bernard. "I have not questioned my faith as you suggest. I do not believe the Church abandons God's business by also dealing in the business of man. Abelard's trial may be the first of many designed to purge the Church's ranks of heretics and blasphemers such as him. I would not want to be counted among them if I were you."

"I have no fear of what you think you can do to me," said Peter resolutely.

"Make sure your vote truly considers the well-being of the Church and not just a method to appease your own conscience that such derogation from the faith as Abelard's, and now yours just confessed, is justifiable," warned Bernard.

"I have no more allegiance to Abelard than I do to you, only to the truth. I may not know what vote I'll cast until my hand finishes the last stroke, but I tell you this, my decision will not be based on threats or petty attempts at self-aggrandisement." He looked sternly at Lotulpt and me and then left the room.

"At worst that is only one vote," commented Lotulpt disdainfully.

"Lotulpt, keep on the high road with your allegations or we may lose the support of more important people than just your fellow judges," cautioned Bernard. "Popular opinion can be fickle as a young maiden with too many suitors. If one errs, another gains favour."

We left the room and returned to our seats. The crowd seemed to be tiring from the long drawn-out affair. Bernard sensed their restlessness and decided to end the debate.

"Are there any more questions for Abelard?" he asked of the judges.

"Yes, I have one last question," replied Peter to the surprise of us all. He rose from his table, walked to the centre of the interrogation area, and sat on the wooden bench placed there earlier for Abelard to sit upon but who, instead, had remained standing in place during the entire proceeding.

Peter then softly posed his question, "Abelard, the Holy Catholic Church believes it has maintained the continuous transmission of Christ's ministry from the day Jesus chose Saint Peter to be the head of his Church, to the present day, by affirming that each pope is a direct successor of Saint Peter. This doctrine gives the Church the right and duty to set rules, teach morals, and exact obedience so that the authority and spiritual gifts operative in the days of the apostles remain operative today. If someone deviates from this doctrine by calling into question the authority and traditions of the Church, is that not then, by its very definition, heresy?"

Abelard sat down next to Peter and answered in equal voice, "The continued legitimacy of the Church's authority is only guaranteed by the continued presence of the Holy Spirit, La Paraclète, within the Church. If the Spirit is shut out by cupidity and lust for power, by human vices and devices, by pedantry and intolerant dogma, then the Church relinquishes its authority because the Spirit has moved on to become manifest in other ways as simple as the caring of one person for another. Was that not the lesson of Christ?" Peter remained silent and looked closely at Abelard before getting up to return to his chair.

A quiet had overtaken the assembled company. "Had Daniel once again emerged unscathed from the lions' den?" I wondered.

Bernard broke the silence. "All right, if there are no more questions, we should conclude this business. Judges, you four have each been given the opportunity to interrogate Abelard, review his works, and have read rebuttals of his teachings by scholastics from the abbey of Saint Victor. The decision is yours whether or not this Council should recommend to Rome that his works are condemnable as heresy and that the man, Abelard, should be recommended for condemnation as well since works are inseparable from the man." He motioned to the cleric beside him who immediately got up from his chair. "Upon these ballots being passed out, you will make one of two marks," instructed Bernard. "An 'X' is the sign for condemnation, and an 'O' will be the mark of absolution. Carefully weigh the matter when casting your vote and keep in mind that God is entrusting you with the preservation of his Church through your decision."

All were silent, and none of us moved to make the first mark. I am convinced that Lotulpt was simply refraining from making his mark too quickly as a show of judicious deliberation, but finally he was the first to fold his ballot and return it to the cleric. I was second. My heart was pounding so hard that I thought it would surely be heard throughout the chamber as, with sweaty hand, I slid my vote to the edge of the table for it to be collected with the others. Peter was staring off into some fathomless distance. He had hardly moved since returning to his seat. It appeared as if he was trying to absorb the answer from some unknown power. Never changing his far-focused gaze, he wrote upon the ballot and handed it to the waiting cleric.

I had not been paying much attention to Fulbert. His ballot was in his hand, yet I did not know if it was still as he had received it or if he had finished putting his mark upon it. The cleric came and stood in front of him.

"Master Fulbert," prodded the monk, "Your ballot please."

With hardly a sound, Fulbert slipped out of his seat and onto the floor. His eyes were tense and rigid but his body was relaxed and limp. Héloïse rushed from the crowd and to his side. On the floor beside him she cradled his head in her lap and repeatedly cooed, "Dear, sweet uncle."

"Héloïse," mouthed Fulbert in a barely audible voice. He turned his head to look toward her with eyes that could barely see, blinked once, and then tightly closed his eyes forever.

Abelard went over to Héloïse, knelt beside her, and spoke comfortingly to her, "God gave him sight to see the one he loved most for a last time. It is the vision he most desired to capture and carry with him into heaven."

"What about his vote?" interrupted Lotulpt as he pointed to the piece of paper clutched in the dying man's hand.

Héloïse's incessant glare at Lotulpt was as sharp as a dagger while she gently pried loose the folded paper from her uncle's possession. She opened it so that she alone could see what had been written upon it and broke into what I thought were tears of distress. Then, to everyone's amazement she stood and triumphantly lifted up high for all to see what Fulbert had scrawled upon his ballot. "It is an 'O'!" she said defiantly to Bernard. Sure enough, on that piece of paper Fulbert's trembling hand had drawn an "O" as large as the paper could contain, and within that circle an ichthys, the sign of the fish, the symbol of our Lord, Jesus Christ, the forgiver of all our sin.

Héloïse gave Abelard a long hug. It was the first time since their parting that they had physically touched one another, and probably the last. In her mind, and by her count, Abelard had been vindicated.

Bernard stood and directed people to assist with Fulbert. "Do not let a great man die upon the floor," he ordered. "Take him to my chambers and administer the rights he is so worthily due." Six men lifted the frail body of Fulbert to shoulder height while another supported his dangling head as they carried him through the crowd. Some knelt and others bowed as he passed. Many in the crowd had been his pupil, and from them especially were silent tears shed.

Later, in the cathedral's guest chamber bed, clergy laid Fulbert prone on his back on clean linen sheets and in fresh robes. Bernard himself crossed Fulbert's arms over his chest to cradle a golden crucifix. For almost two days Fulbert waited motionless on death while incense was burned and a constant flow of admirers filed through the room to pay their last respects.

After the crowd had settled from the distraction of Fulbert's collapse, Bernard continued with the polling of the vote. "Counting Fulbert's vote, it seems that there is a tie," he pronounced. "The task then falls to me to break the tie."

"Let me see the other ballots!" insisted Héloïse.

"You dare impugn my honour?" Bernard retorted. "I will not have my authority be so challenged. The vote is as I announced it."

"Show her the ballots," spoke Peter as he rose from his seat and approached Bernard.

Bernard quickly turned over the three ballots he was holding for everyone to see and revealed the two "X's" and one "O" he had accurately reported. "Remove the woman from this place," he commanded loudly. Two monks approached Héloïse threateningly, but Peter intervened.

"Leave her alone," he said quietly and the monks obeyed. Peter then motioned for Thessaly to come up to Héloïse's side. "Take her to be with her uncle," he told Thessaly. "She has done all she can do here."

Never taking her eyes off Abelard, Héloïse backed out of the cathedral at Thessaly's continued prodding. Abelard never took his eyes off her until the closing of the cathedral's heavy doors broke their visual connection.

"Abelard," called Bernard. Abelard turned around. "Abelard, I will not shirk my duty as a responsible leader of the Church. No matter how much we might emotionally want to absolve you, the simple truth is that your writing is intentionally heretical. Therefore, by casting my vote with the other two who marked the sign of the 'X' upon their ballot, I hereby condemn your works as heresy and henceforth declare that the reading, reciting, and the referencing of your written word is likewise heresy and shall be dealt with accordingly. Further, my recommendation to Rome is that you personally warrant condemnation and censure for your actions, and that you must cease further lecturing, teaching, and writing. And, if you do not desist from doing so, you should receive permanent excommunication from the Holy Roman Catholic Church, without absolution even unto death, to face eternal damnation."

Abelard showed no visible reaction to Bernard's condemnation.

Bernard continued, "Yet, to show you that the Church is compassionate, that this condemnation is meant to be redemptive rather than punitive, it has been decided to utilise your administrative talents as abbot of St. Gildas de Rhuys in Brittany. There you will be immediately taken and remain until such time as your penance is complete or as suits the needs of the Church."

An armed escort came up beside Abelard to march him out of the cathedral. There was a mixed reaction from the crowd as he passed by. Some jeered and shouted, "Heretic!" while others offered quiet words of encouragement.

Stepping over to Peter, I made the observation, "It has been a long-fought battle between Bernard and Abelard. For both of them, I am glad it is at last over."

Ignoring my comment, Peter called out loudly the words by which Jesus charged his disciples, "Beware of men; for they will deliver you up to councils, and flog you in their synagogues."

Chapter Fourteen

A Soul Released

*T*hose who abide by this shall find happiness and fulfilment in their lives.

I was awakened by the first words Abelard had uttered in almost two days. "It is finished," he sighed as if exorcising all the anguish from a tortured soul. Here ended Abelard's story, his *Historia Calamitatum*, here in the confines of St. Gildas abbey, where neither friend nor foe could have released him from his self-made prison. He set his pen down on the easel and read his final script,

> *"The great goodness of God permits nothing to be done without reason, and brings to good end whatsoever may seem to happen wrongfully. Even such are those who yield to their own rather than to the divine purpose, and with hidden desires resist the spirit which echoes in the words, 'Thy will be done,' thus placing their own will ahead of the will of God. Farewell."*

He then turned to a page in the Bible next to him, and read from the book of Corinthians,

*"Blessed be the God and Father of our Lord Jesus
Christ, the Father of mercies and God of all comfort,
who comforts us in all our affliction, so that we may
be able to comfort those in affliction, with the comfort
with which we ourselves are comforted by God."*

I was startled when he then spoke directly to me,
"Alberic," he said, "Those who understand and keep in
perspective their own sufferings and setbacks are in a position
to comfort others."

Flipping a few more pages further into the Book, he read
aloud again,

*"Indeed, I count everything as loss because of the
surpassing worth of knowing Christ Jesus my Lord.
For his sake I have suffered the loss of all things, and
count them as refuse, in order that I may gain Christ
and be found in him."*

"Alberic," he said again, "Those who count nothing as loss,
not birthright, nor fame, or earthly wisdom, gain everything.
Every experience of life, good or bad, has value and meaning
and, by knowing that, one controls his or her own destiny."

Still from Saint Paul's letter to the Philippians, Abelard
continued reading another passage,

*"Finally, brethren, whatever is true, whatever is
honourable, whatever is just, whatever is pure,
whatever is lovely, whatever is gracious, if there is
any excellence, if there is anything worthy of praise,
think about these things."*

"Alberic," he said once more, "Those who abide by this
shall find happiness and fulfilment in their lives."

I was very weary and desirous of rest, so I told him, "Abelard, I must go."

"So soon?" he asked.

Abelard had languished at St. Gildas far too long. Bernard had prevailed upon Pope Innocent II to condemn Abelard and, so, he had remained banished to this loathsome place. Abelard, too, was exhausted. He had not slept nor eaten since my arrival. Even though during my visit I had managed to sleep on occasion and had nourished myself with the meagre provisions I had originally brought for the trip, Abelard had not allowed himself to indulge often in such comforts for a long time. Why would I want to stay under such conditions?

Abelard hurriedly packed his manuscript into a leather satchel and shoved it into my arms. "Take this, and share it with all who may be comforted by it," he said in a commanding voice.

"You should keep it and give it to someone more deserving," I protested. Any of Abelard's writing was still considered heresy, even something as innocuous as this short autobiography. I was not sure I wanted to be the possessor of it, but it seemed I had little choice.

"You *are* deserving," he said slowly and emphatically.

He walked me to the doorway of the scriptorium. He placed his hand upon my cheek. "Goodbye, old friend," he said almost in a whisper.

As I turned away to leave down the shadowy hallway, the darkness before me seemed thick and smothering. I turned back to say something to Abelard, but I could not utter a word.

He waited a moment and then, with eyes aglow, he stated, "If Christ could forgive even as the spikes were being driven through his hands, how could I do less?"

I turned away from his gaze as tears began pouring down my face. Quickly composing myself, I turned back again to see him one last time, but he was gone, and the vesper bell rang nine.

Shortly after my visit at St. Gildas, I heard that Abelard had set off alone for Rome to appeal his condemnation. Had I only known, had he simply asked, I would have gone with him. He was in no physical condition to make such a trip. He only made it as far south as Cluny. Peter put him up in residency at a priory associated with his abbey near Chalon-sur-Saône. While there, Peter shared with Abelard a prized accomplishment, the first translation of the Qur'an from Arabic into Latin. On sabbatical to Spain, Peter had commissioned the translation and then brought it to his abbey for scrupulous study. It is said that Abelard died in Peter's arms while the abbot was reading this passage from the book to him,

> *"Knows he not that when the contents of the graves are brought out and poured forth, that which is in the breasts of men shall be made known. Verily, that Day their Lord will be well-acquainted with them."*

Surprisingly, Bernard had gone to visit Abelard at Cluny before he died, and through Peter's influence, some believe the two were reconciled. Before leaving, Bernard even left funds for Abelard's burial expenses at Cluny.

Actually, I heard about all this when subsequently visiting Héloïse. After a visit to either Abelard or Héloïse, I would generally visit the other as soon as possible to pass along welcomed information between the two. Those occasions had become less and less frequent over the years, but this visit proved especially timely for Héloïse.

"Quickly," Héloïse urged, "Travel to Cluny and retrieve Abelard's body. I have summoned John, who has gone on a trip, but I fear he will be too late. Implore Peter to let Abelard rest in his beloved and hallowed ground of La Paraclète."

Here demonstrates the difference between God and man. Where were the loyal followers? Abelard's disciples all fled upon his condemnation and never returned. His works are forgotten. He is forgotten. I, alone, was left to take care of matters.

With borrowed donkey and cart, I travelled the distance to Cluny via the shortest route I knew. The evening upon my arrival, Peter and I loaded the wrapped body of Abelard onto the wagon and covered it completely with straw. It would not have bode well for me if the authorities caught me with the corpse, so its concealment was of utmost importance. Thoughtful of the journey ahead, Peter added some fragrant melons to the wagon's cargo to overpower any telltale odour exuding from Abelard's spoiling body.

I delivered my load to Héloïse and left her to her business. I saw her not much after that. In fact, during the two decades between Abelard's death and her own, it was no more than a handful of times that we saw one another. The convent of La Paraclète struggled after Abelard's death. Without his imposing presence and influence, there were fewer generous benefactors to support the convent. Crops failed. Many nuns loyal to Héloïse passed on with no new converts to replace them. John worked as hard as he could as carpenter, mason, field hand, and general caretaker to preserve the place, but he did not have the persuasive abilities of Abelard to obtain commitment from those who had the wherewithal to save the convent. After long service to the convent, John's only reward was to die cradled in the bosom of Héloïse.

Eventually, the convent became irretrievably impoverished, yet Héloïse would not acknowledge it. She once told me, "As long as La Paraclète remains, Abelard is eternal and he is with me." She carried on, as she always had, undeterred by all Abelard had thrust upon her.

At my final visit to an aged and ailing Héloïse, she implored, "Lay me by my love. Do that one thing for me, Alberic."

"Had I not done enough already..." I thought.

I stayed in the guest chamber of the convent for nearly a month while Héloïse's sisters in Christ attended daily to her final needs. When the fateful day came, one of the nuns reported to me that Héloïse's breathing had gotten ever so shallow and that the interval between her breaths had gotten ever so long. Her eyes had become fixed in a distant gaze. No more could someone speak to her and expect a response. I went to see her.

Left alone in the room with Héloïse, I pondered many things. I posed to myself the question as to how our lives might have been different if fate had headed us down other pathways. I spoke to her more that day than during any other day of my life. I told her of thoughts that had long pervaded my mind of which I had never dared tell her, or anyone, before, or after, that time. "Perhaps," I mused, "You were the one person in my life whom I truly loved."

And then she died. Without ever gaining her favour, without ever knowing even sisterly love, she left me. Yet, somehow I felt better for having told her all those things.

Epilogue

Exhumation ad extremum

*T*he great day will come when not our bodies will be exhumed from the grave, but, instead, our motives, by which we will all be judged.

The old man still sitting across the table from me rested rigidly back into his chair – "And that is what has brought us to this place tonight," he said, "To fulfil the final tasks put upon me. One was to lay Héloïse to rest beside Abelard, and another was to tell this story."

Standing up to stretch his tired muscles, Alberic made a final editorial remark, "Witnessing such calamity, one sometimes wonders what could have been done to prevent it, however it is evident that the two of them share the responsibility for their misfortunes with no others."

There was no need for me to make any comment.

"Only one task more remains," he began. "A long time ago a promise was made to see to your upbringing. As an infant, you were set up to lead a privileged life in the home of a wealthy Parisian merchant, and he treated you as a son as your father had treated his. Your life was so blissful that it needed little interference from me. Now, interfere I must, for a proper upbringing requires learning the truth about oneself, painful though it may be." He picked up the manuscript and returned it to the satchel. "So that, as I suffered, you do not have to go through life without knowing your kin, I am compelled to reveal to you that the author of this work is your father."

"And my mother was his beloved Héloïse," I stated bluntly.

He looked at me with incredulity. "I did not know you knew this," he replied with some embarrassment evident in his voice. Alberic tightly tied the leather bands of the satchel to secure its contents.

"I knew my parents well, from boyhood to manhood. They visited me individually, never together, and wrote to me regularly. My father saw to my education by securing the finest teachers for me and through personal mentoring. I was an heir to his family's sizable estate. The Church, for want of money to do good things, could have been bought by his wealth, but Abelard would have none of that. Instead, he used the money to ensure my future. My mother attended me if I was ill and comforted me if I was hurting. They were never far from my side either in body or spirit, and I knew they loved me, and each other. I suffered not for want of loving kinsmen."

"Then that is your luxury, for some are not so fortunate," Alberic said as he tried to wipe off with hand and spit the dust that had become engrained in the leather baggage he had been carrying for so long.

"Except for brief visits convenient to you, when we amicably argued and debated subjects of interest to you, where were you?" I asked.

He made no answer.

"Lo, here is the true exhumation of this night. You have had loving father, friends, and kin, but you chose not to abide them. You did not laugh or cry with them in life, or mourn with them or at their passing. The spirit moves within us, but it also moves among us. The interconnection between us is the spirit, and the spirit is what interconnects us. Yet the energy of the spirit moving among us is what so many are unable to tap because they harbour envy, seek vengeance, and crave earthly power and fame and fortune above all else. Therefore, the spirit is lost to them and they become an imprisoned soul."

He dropped the satchel hard upon the table. "I did not summon you here to preach to me," he complained.

"The great day will come when not our bodies will be exhumed from the grave, but, instead, our motives, by which we will all be judged."

Alberic returned to his chair and we sat silently for a moment. I felt sorrow for the man now sitting slumped at the table opposite me. He never understood his closest friends and his life was controlled by emotions that prevented him access to truth and love. Despite his objection to Abelard's definition of sin, through him my father's words proved nonetheless correct. The world may deem Alberic's life and actions as moral and good, even commendable. However, the consent of his mind to do what he knew was wrong was crushing him by the ensuing sense of guilt that bore heavily upon him, and this burden had become even weightier as the years wore on.

Breaking the silence that we had uncomfortably sustained, Alberic finally said, "You know, some of those who perpetrated the crime against Abelard were punished by losing their eyes and genitalia." He paused a moment and then added, "Why not all?"

"I suppose that justice is dispensed differently upon thugs for hire and thugs of misguided conscience," I philosophized.

He nodded.

"Should it end here," I wondered to myself. "Can there be release for this man? Am I the instrument to pierce his heart or mend it?" I decided to proceed with his delicate surgery by saying, "I will at least not let you die fatherless as your father died sonless."

"I have long suspected my father's identity," he said without much emotion. "It became obvious when Fulbert treated niece like nephew. By Fulbert's hand, Héloïse's early life and mine ran so parallel that it betrayed the fact that I was her illegitimate sibling. Along with the fact that, 'Alberic' means 'having the nature of Alber,' or 'little Alber,' and that 'Alber' is the root for both the name of the father and the child, there lies the convincing link to my father, Albertus, and my sister, Héloïse."

"Alas, old man, not father, only uncle, and sister not even half! And legitimate as well, for your father was married to your mother, but had not revealed it because your father's father would have thought the bride beneath his son's station. Fulbert so loved his brother that he named his only son after him."

Alberic was visibly shaken. He sunk deeper into his chair. "How do you know this?" he quietly asked.

"I got to know my great uncle well. He told me stories, wonderful stories that I begged him to often repeat. Through his own words I discovered that Fulbert knew passionate love; Fulbert knew murderous rage, even against his own father. That is why he could not condemn Abelard. That is why he could not disclose himself to a son who would not understand such transgressions."

"And yet, apparently, he entrusted others with such knowledge," Alberic said with bitterness. "I would have thought he would have considered whose life would be most affected by the divulging of it."

"Whose life did you live anyway?" I replied in Fulbert's defence. "Certainly not your own; you wrote history while others made it. You projected your life into other people's lives and pretended it was your own. You seemed to care not about your own story unless to moan about it, so why should Fulbert have added to your misery?"

"I guess that was my life, as much as it was, if you say so," retorted the old man.

Picking up the satchel from the table, I stood and announced, "I will relieve you of this burden, for my father's work was meant to be shared, not coveted."

"Good riddance, for his work has been nothing but a curse upon me," complained Alberic.

"Poor wretch," I thought, "You have been cursed far worse than all those whose misfortunes you previously mentioned, for they have lost their life but once, while you have lost it daily by never living it."

I wondered if it would serve any further purpose to disclose to my cousin-german that the item he had carefully guarded for so long was nothing more than paper and ink - not a document of indictment, heresy, or intrigue that needed to be secreted away. Unbeknownst to Alberic, who slept while the document was being penned, Abelard had made a duplicate of his manuscript and the copy had been widely distributed among his friends and followers. His dear Heloise read the manuscript with sympathetic eyes and regarded its candid content as a just condemnation of the atrocities brought upon her honourable husband. Perhaps she was less forgiving than Abelard when she wrote her response to his manuscript:

> *"After setting forth thy former prosecution by thy masters, then the outrage of supreme treachery upon thy body, thou has turned thy pen to the execrable jealousy and inordinate assaults of thy fellow-pupils, namely Alberic of Rheims and Lotulpt the Lombard; and what by their instigation was done to that famous work of thy theology, and what to thyself, as it were condemned to prison, thou has not omitted."*

Abelard had not intended to invoke vengeance upon Alberic through his writing. He had compassionately given one copy of his manuscript to Alberic in hope that it might be an aid and comfort to him as he faced his own dilemmas and trials of life. I doubt he ever read it. Instead of beleaguering the point, I decided to try to exhibit the same compassion as my father by pursuing a kinder discourse.

"Because we love one another we have passed from death into life," I told him. "That is what I learned this night when you took me to the edge of the grave." I walked around to his side of the table and put both hands upon his shoulders. "It is with love that I have said all of these things to you, love that I share with you as kinsman, and love I convey to you from your kinsmen now departed." I kissed him on the top of his head. He slipped still further down into his chair to such an extent that I feared he might soon fall to the floor. From behind, I grabbed him under his arms and lifted him back into his seat.

I then departed from the old man's company, closed the outside door of his quarters behind me, and there met a nun with bent and fragile frame who had been patiently waiting at the door. "Still watching over him, Thessaly?" I asked.

"Someone has to care for the old fool," she replied with a kindly smile upon her wrinkled face.

"For how long can you bear it?" I wondered aloud while giving the sweet old woman a hug.

"Till I lay him in his grave, Astrolabe, till I lay him in his grave," she said with quivering voice. "Even he deserves embracing when he breathes his last." She went in to check on Alberic.

The greatest of all human attributes is love, and somehow sacrificial love always finds a way to triumph over any evil. How could Alberic not recognize such love as from the old woman who so unwearyingly waited upon him? How he could ever construe the lives of my mother and father as anything but a story of enduring and sacrificial love, I could not understand. However, as it would have been to my beloved parents, this quandary or his personal actions were not going to allow him to be a cause and effect upon my life by abiding any vindictiveness toward this pathetic old soul.

I looked out across the horizon. Was it daybreak already? No, it was false dawn; a time when there seems to be light coming over the world, but when there is still much darkness before the light truly comes forth. Yet through the clouds and prevailing gloom of night, high in the sky where men cannot corrupt, the brilliance of the stars remain everlasting and undimmed.

About The Author

Rod Randall is a graduate of Elmhurst College where he majored in Political Science and Urban Studies. He attended the University of Virginia's Woodrow Wilson School of Government and, later, studied Public Administration at the University of Illinois. He, eventually, took over the operation of his family's business.

Rod has been involved with many organizations from President of the Elmhurst College Alumni Association to Committee Chairman of the local Boy Scout troop. As a trustee of his local library district, he served as Building Chairman where he oversaw the design and construction of a new library for his hometown community of Arthur.

Except for a few poems, Rod is unpublished even though he has been writing for years as a hobby. In college, he minored in Speech and Theatre and wrote one-act plays. Recently, he wrote and directed a full-length play called *Future Reminiscence* to celebrate his community's 125th anniversary of its founding. The play took the audience 25 years into the future to envision how events today would affect the town of tomorrow.

Rod Randall – 412 N Vine, Arthur, IL 61911
Phone: (217) 543-3133 Fax: (217) 543-3534
email: randall@arthur.k12.il.us

The author wishes to acknowledge gratefully the immeasurable assistance he received from his editor, *Roxane Christ*, whose patient encouragement helped bring this work to faster and fuller fruition.

Printed in the United States
29772LVS00001B/58-159